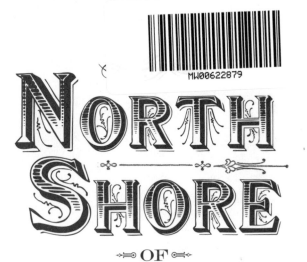

NORTH SHORE

OF

Massachusetts Bay

An
Illustrated
Guide
AND
History

Benjamin D. Hill & Winfield S. Nevins

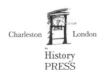

Charleston   London

The
History
PRESS

Published by The History Press
Charleston, SC 29403
www.historypress.net

Copyright © 2008 The History Press
All rights reserved

Originally published 1881
The History Press edition 2008

Manufactured in the United Kingdom

ISBN 978.1.59629.440.0

Library of Congress CIP data applied for.

From the Publisher:
This new edition contains the full text from the original 1881 fourth edition
of *The North Shore of Massachusetts Bay, An Illustrated Guide*. Some of the
advertisements that appeared in the original have been deleted or moved from
their original placements.

Notice: The information in this book is true and complete to the best of our
knowledge. It is offered without guarantee on the part of The History Press.
The History Press disclaims all liability in connection with the use of this book.

The History Press is proud to reissue this nineteenth-century classic. This new edition of The North Shore of Massachusetts Bay, An Illustrated Guide *contains the full text of the fourth edition of the guidebook and some of the advertisements that appeared in the 1881 publication.*

It is our hope that you will enjoy this charming volume as you explore and discover the treasures of the North Shore.

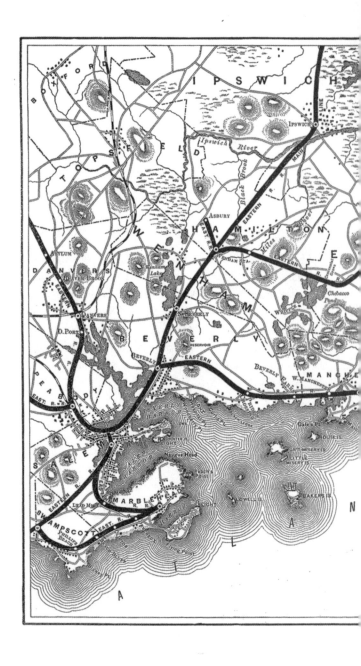

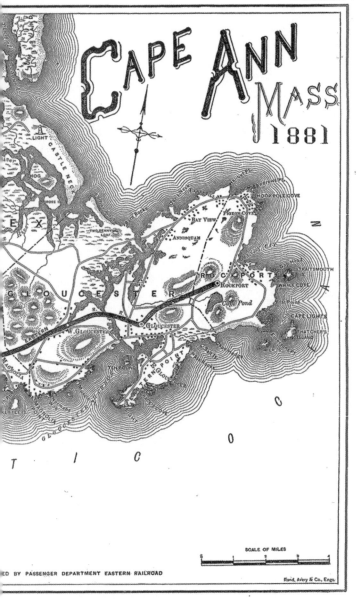

CAPE ANN

MASS.

1881

SCALE OF MILES

ED BY PASSENGER DEPARTMENT EASTERN RAILROAD

Reid, Avery & Co., Engs.

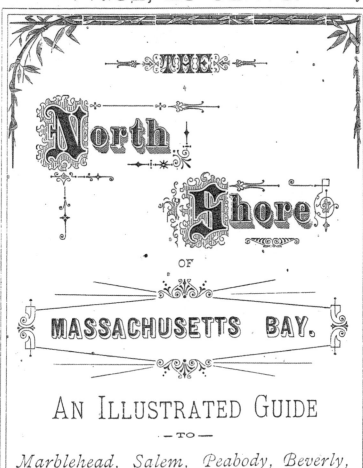

THE

North Shore

OF

MASSACHUSETTS BAY.

AN ILLUSTRATED GUIDE

— TO —

Marblehead, Salem, Peabody, Beverly,
Manchester=by=the=Sea, Magnolia,
Gloucester, Rockport,
and Ipswich.

By Benj. D. Hill and Winfield S. Nevins.

—·— **FOURTH EDITION.** —·—

SALEM, MASS., 1881.

INTRODUCTORY.

When Roger Conant, that observing pioneer, sailed along the Cape shore from Gloucester to the mouth of the Naumkeag river, he saw the coast was one of no common beauty. To his penetrating glance was revealed a landscape of fresh and charming lines,—the foreground a picturesque coast, the distance filled by undulating hills that lay soft hidden in the blue of a bright summer morning. Conant was delighted. Seeking a spot where religion should be as free as the air around, could he do better than to plant a colony where every influence of nature seconded his pious purpose ? Intolerance and bigotry could hardly find place where every idling wind placed its veto on slavery to anything. Conant needed no second thought, and with the readiness of a man who appreciates, he at once moved a portion of his little colony to the mouth of the Naumkeag.

What Roger Conant gloried in two hundred and fifty years ago, strikes the observer to-day with the same gentle force ; whether he sails along the coast, or travels the centre of the Cape by the Eastern railway to Salem, Marblehead, and Beverly harbors, acres of tiny forests, little villas like diamonds in rich natural settings, broad and undulating fields, glimpses of the sea, each and all contribute to paint a picture for the traveler that can scarce fade from his memory.

From Newport to Portland a more dainty bit of natural beauty it would be hard to find. And visitors to the north

shore of Massachusetts bay, let them come when they may,
never leave it without the resolve to return. How charmingly Higginson has written of it in his Oldport Days, and
yet the immortality conferred on it there has not made it
known to the large mass of readers ; for Higginson wrote
as a poet, and the practical part, the unpoetical part of this
life, is wanting. Had he supplied this, no special pleading
for our beloved cape would have been needed. And
while we do not presume to place ourselves on a level with
that distinguished writer, we trust the work we submit to
the public in all modesty, may fill their needs, and satisfy
their thirst for knowledge. Woven with a description of
the localities the reader will find the more interesting
events of their histories, and, while not overlooking the
needs and certain aims of a guide book, we have endeav-
ored to obliterate as much as possible the dry matter-of-
factness of such productions.

PREFACE TO FOURTH EDITION. This work was first
issued in May, 1879 ; a second edition was issued the same
season, and a third edition in May, 1880. We now submit
the fourth edition. The work has been substantially re-
written for this edition, and with each issue our endeavor
has been to correct, revise, and improve. The map which
accompanies the book this year, and for which we are in-
debted to Mr. Lucius Tuttle of the Eastern railway, will
be found a great improvement over that of 1880.

SALEM, May, 1881.

MARBLEHEAD.

Its History — Old Landmarks — Clifton House — The Neck.

As the reader of this book turns over leaf after leaf and recurs to the brief historical sketches of the towns along the North Shore, he will note one peculiar fact in connection with each, and one common to all. It is this: These towns which are now popular summer resorts for the wealthy people of Boston and elsewhere, were once fishing ports and the abodes of that humble yeomanry who fight the battle of life amid greater perils than those which surround the soldier himself. Especially is this true of Marblehead. This old town has a romantic history, and even to this day there is a tinge of romance surrounding its every day life as there is of picturesqueness overshadowing it topographically, It was deeded to the white men by the Indians in 1684, for the sum of £14, 13s. It was incorporated on May 2, 1649, as "Marble Harbor," and is, therefore, one of the oldest towns in New England. Previous to this it formed a part of Salem. Very little fishing is now done by its citizens, the principal industries being market-gardening, and the manufacture of boots and shoes. Marblehead is a grand old town, and has a record for devotion to the cause of liberty, of patriotism, and of courage unsurpassed in history. The following interesting description of some objects of interest is from "Old Naumkeag":

"One of the curiosities of the village is its crooked, meandering streets. The town was evidently settled without regard to streets or boundary lines, each settler locating on some ledge or rise of ground, wherever he pleased. Marblehead is rich in landmarks of the past. There is the Mugford monument on Pleasant street near the Eastern depot; the Soldiers' and Sailors' monument on Mugford street; the old North church, rich in historic associations; St. Michael's church, built in 1714, still in a good state of preservation, and serving the Episcopalians of Marblehead as a place of worship, and whose second pastor, the Rev. David Mosson, subsequently moving to Virginia, had the distinguished honor of marrying George Washington and Mrs. Martha Custis. Also, the town house, built in 1727, on the spot where the " gaol and cage" once stood; the old powder house; parson Barnard's old residence, built in 1720; the house in which Elbridge Gerry was born; the birthplace and early home of Judge Story; the early home of good old parson Holyoke who left Marblehead to take charge of Harvard college and win fresh laurels; the old burial ground with its quaint tomb-stones bearing the oddest of inscriptions. Then there is the famous old Lee house, built by Hon. Jeremiah Lee at a cost of £10,000. It was magnificently finished and some remains of its former grandeur may be seen to-day in its spacious hall, carved wainscotings and beautiful historic paper hangings. Towering above all these monuments of the past is the new Abbot Hall, a bequest from a generous native of the town, BENJAMIN ABBOT. Mr. Abbot's bequest amounted to over $100,000, and the hall cost $75,000. The sum of $20,000 was set apart for a public library and reading room, of which strangers may enjoy all privileges by depositing $3 as security." In the Abbot Hall reading room are several paintings of unusual merit, especially the famous "Yankee Doodle," and in the main hall one of Mr. Abbot.

On the outskirts of the village is the Devereux mansion, where Longfellow wrote, in 1849, "Fire of Driftwood":

> "We sat within the farm-house old,
>   Whose windows looking o'er the bay,
> Gave to the sea-breeze, damp and cold,
>   An easy entrance night and day.
>
> Not far away we saw the port,
>   The strange, old fashioned, silent town,
> The lighthouse, the dismantled fort,
>   The wooden houses, quaint and brown.

The windows, rattling in their frames,
The ocean roaring up the beach,
The gusty blast, the bickering flames,
All mingled with our speech."

As a summer resort, Marblehead has no superior on the
Atlantic coast. Its bold and rocky shores extending far out
into the open sea, its cool, pure and invigorating.air, its irreg-
ular cliffs, its green fields, its beautiful slopes and its pleasant
roads, make it a delightful retreat for such as seek genuine
rest and recreation.

The peninsula known as Marblehead Great Neck is one and
a quarter miles in length, and about a half a mile in width at
the widest point. Just before the first gun of the Revolution
was fired a company of "British regulars" was stationed on
its heights to overawe the people of the town and to compel
compliance with the restrictions which the British government
was attempting to enforce. But although the place was cool
and airy, the Marblehead boys who afterward composed the
"amphibious regiment" of Col. Glover made it so uncomfort-
ably warm for them that they soon deemed it expedient to
evacuate. The Neck is connected with the main land by a
narrow isthmus, along which the sea itself has constructed one
of the firmest foundations for a highway by washing up a vast
line of boulders. In a storm the sea beats upon the ocean side
with tremendous force. There can hardly be conceived a
grander sight than is witnessed on this neck when a south-
easter gets at work in earnest. The ledges exposed to the
ocean are high, and in several places channels have been worn,
into which the water is driven in storms with such tremendous
force as to throw the spray often more than one hundred feet
into the air. The Neck is bounded on the one side by Massachusetts bay and on the other side by Marblehead harbor,
and comprises every variety of shore.

The harbor, on the northwesterly side, between the Neck
and the village, is a half mile wide and is one of the best
yacht harbors on the coast. This fact has brought many
yachtsmen here to live and made the Neck the headquarters of
the Eastern yacht club, which built a club-house here during

1880. The view across the harbor is charming by day or night. The quaint old town on its eternal foundation is the extreme of picturesque, and reminds one of some ancient Italian villa nestling on the banks of the Mediterranean and backed by bold bluffs surmounted by a noble castle of the days of yore. There too, are those sombre old Marblehead wharves, as solid as the foundation on which stands the town. There, also, to the eastward, is Peach's point, and on one side of it Fort Sewall, still maintained as a fortification under the care of a gentlemanly sergeant. The view along the coast and out to sea is grand in the extreme, taking in a full sweep of the ocean. On the harbor side are Beverly, Manchester-by-the-Sea, and Gloucester, with their variations of beach, bluff, and sloping bank, the light-houses on Thatcher's island, and Eastern point, while as the eye sweeps to the south it rests on Hospital point, and Baker's island, Marblehead Neck light itself, Egg rock, and Minot's ledge lights, and the outer lights of Boston harbor. Swampscott, Lynn, and Nahant fade away to the west and south into the dimly seen South Shore.

The bathing facilities are very good, although there is no high rolling surf. As for fishing, the sea perch may be caught from almost any point on the shore, and cod and other large fish by rowing a short distance. The drives both on the Neck and about the town generally, are very fine. A splendid highway encircles the entire territory of the Neck, affording one of the grandest drives on the New England coast. On the main land the roads through Marblehead, Swampscott, Lynn, Nahant, along Atlantic avenue, Ocean street, and Nahant beach can hardly be surpassed in attractiveness. In the other direction the drives to Salem, where all its historic points may be visited, thence along the Beverly and Cape Ann shore, are equally pleasant.

Marblehead Neck, as a summer resort, is of about twenty years' growth, attention having been called to its exceptionally favorable location for health, seclusion and comfort about 1860. No great amount of building was done during the next ten years, only a few small cottages being erected each year. Mrs. E. D. Kimball of Salem was the first to erect a large residence, about 1873, and since then there has been a steady improvement in the character of the cottages. The growth of the settlement has been remarkably rapid during the last four or five years.

Finely made roads lead around and across the Neck; the lots are laid out on a liberal scale and the shore is reserved to public uses; no purchaser of shore lots having control of the immediate beaches or cliffs. The greater part of the land formerly belonged to the estate of the late Ephraim Brown, and the remainder to Isaac C. Wyman, Esq., who is now one of the trustees of the Brown property, together with Hon. William D. Northend and George F. Flint, Esq. For some time the sale of building sites and the settlement of the place was suspended on account of disputed claims. But full settlement of all controversies was made in 1878, and under the energetic management of the trustees named, sales of building lots to the amount of more than $100,000 have been made since October, 1877. Many of the best lots still remain in the market and may be purchased at rates within the means of the average summer resident at the sea-shore.

It has been and is the desire of the trustees that the estate be sold in good sized lots, so that the place may not become too crowded for comfort; but smaller lots are sold in particular sections. The distance from the entrance upon the Neck to Devereux station on the Swampscott branch railway is about three-quarters of a mile. Barges connect with all the trains during the summer months, and Capt. E. A. Pitman runs a fine new steamer from the village across the harbor almost hourly, and in connection with all trains to and from Boston and Salem. Trains run to Lynn and Boston over the Swampscott branch and to Salem and points beyond via the Marblehead branch, at frequent intervals; special Marblehead express trains being run to and from Boston. There are a large number of never failing springs of the purest water on the Neck. Ice, milk, vegetables and provisions of all kinds are supplied daily from wagons from the town. The team of I. P. Harris & Co. of Salem visits Marblehead and the Neck daily with every variety of groceries, so that residents can obtain all these supplies without visiting the store at all, and rely upon a prompt attendance to every order. These facilities are among the most attractive of such summer resorts, relieving people of one otherwise unpleasant feature.

The residents have erected a pretty hall or chapel where social gatherings, amusements, and Sunday services find a common temple.   Among the more costly residences are those of Thomas Appleton, W. G. Barker, Mrs. Edward D. Kimball, Edgar Harding, Charles O. Foster, John B. Brown, and W. H. Sweet, the latter costing some $10,000, and one of the finest on the coast.   One of the finest buildings here is the Eastern yacht club house on the harbor side.   It is somewhat of the Elizabethean style and painted bright red.

As we leave the Neck we turn to the left and drive along Atlantic avenue, which leads to Swampscott and Lynn.   The Clifton House is on this avenue near the Swampscott line.

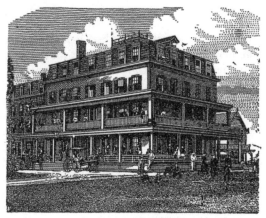

CLIFTON HOUSE.

This is one of the oldest summer resorts on the North Shore and in many respects has few equals.   The location is peculiarly favorable, combining both rocky cliffs and bathing beaches in front, while broad, sloping lawns surround the house on all sides.   Connected with the establishment is one of the best farms in Essex county, and all under the management of the proprietor, Mr. Benj. P. Ware, the president of the Essex County Agricultural society; so that fresh fruit, vegetables and milk, the latter from a herd of premium Ayrshires, are constantly at hand.   Billiard room, bowling alley, and croquet grounds make up the complement.   The stairways and halls have been much improved during the past year, and other beneficial changes have been made.

The view from the piazza of the Clifton is unusually fine, for it overlooks nearly all of Massachusetts bay enlivened by the numerous shipping passing to and from Boston harbor, and also a view of four light-houses. The shores of Nahant, Nantasket and Cohasset are visible, and the various islands of the bay, present, under certain atmospheric conditions, wonderful and beautiful mirage effects resembling the palisades on the Hudson. A particularly interesting feature near the Clifton House, is "gun rock," a singular crevice four feet wide and ten feet deep, extending fifty feet into the rock, through which the waves are forced at times, spouting some sixty feet high. Mr. Ware's post office and telegraphic address is Beach Bluff, Mass.

On the Salem side of the town are the residences of the Crowninshields, Hon. J. J. H. Gregory, and Mr. Ringe, the latter built in 1881.

SALEM.

A CONDENSED GUIDE TO THE CITY.—PLACES AND EVENTS CONNECTED WITH THE WITCHCRAFT ERA.— PUBLIC BUILDINGS AND PLACES.—BUSINESS HOUSES.

WITCHCRAFT. The first inquiry of the tourist on arriving at Salem is for the localities and objects connected with the witchcraft fanaticism. This delusion did not originate in Salem as some people seem to think. As early as 1485, forty-one aged women were burnt in Burlia on similar charges. One inquisition in Piedmont condemned one hundred persons, and in Ravensburg 48; five hundred were executed in Geneva in 1515. There is some authority for saying that witchcraft was a bugbear as early as 1200, and Demonology is almost as old as the human race. English history, from the time of Henry VIII. down to 1712, is filled with accounts of trials and executions for alleged witchcraft manifestations. As late as 1645, ninety persons were hanged under these charges, and previous to that time the usual punishment was burning. Chief Justice Holt was the first judge to protect the accused, and from that moment the superstition declined.* Nor was Salem the first town in the new world where a belief in the superstition took root, for cases occurred in Charlestown and Boston as early as 1648 and 1688. The records of the court at Salem show that from 1652 to 1692 numbers of persons were charged in one form and another with being bewitched. Most of the trials, convictions and executions took place in 1692. There is far more reason for saying that the men who prepared and conducted these infamous proceedings were possessed of the devil, than that their innocent victims were. Neither science, nor theology, nor history, nor "the best light they had in those days," can excuse or palliate the infamy. It was downright fiendishness, in proof of which look at the method of packing the court and conducting the trials.

Among the places of note to be visited in this connection are the following: The *Old Jail*, which stood where Abner C. Goodell's residence now stands on Federal street near St. Peter. Many of the accused were confined here while awaiting a trial which was a mockery, and after trial, while awaiting murder under the forms of law. Some works have stated that Giles Corey was crushed to death here, but Upham says the brutal affair took place in a field. The *Witch House*, so-called, corner Essex and North streets, and sometimes designated the Roger Williams house, and sometimes the Curwin house, was occupied by Williams about 1635. Subsequently it became the property of Judge Curwin. This building obtains its notoriety from the oft repeated assertions that the witch trials occurred here, but they did not. They were held in the court house, on what is now Washington street. It is quite well settled, however, that many of the preliminary examinations of accused persons were held here. The fact that Roger

---

* Pop. Hist. U. S., p. 45, 2–5.

Williams lived in this house is sufficient to render it an object of interest to every one. It is now occupied by a druggist. *Witch Hill*, or *Gallows Hill*, as it is often called, is one mile from the centre of the town and may be reached by horse cars, up Essex street to Nichols. On this hill eighteen or nineteen persons were judicially murdered to satisfy the whims of a few puritan fanatics, for whom there is no more justification than for the authors of the Spanish inquisition, or the tools of Bloody Mary. Bridget Bishop was executed on June 10; Rebecca Nurse, Sarah Goode and probably three others, on July 19; John Willard, Rev. George Burroughs and John Proctor about August 19; Martha Corey, wife of Giles Corey, Ann Pudeator, Alice Parker, and five others on Sept 9, the last executions which took place. In the court house on Federal street are numerous papers connected with witchcraft trials, including the original warrants on which the victims were arrested, tried and executed, and the pins with which the witches are said to have tormented their victims. The trials were held in an old court house which stood at the head of the railroad tunnel near Essex street.

CHURCHES. *The First Church*, corner Washington and Essex streets, is the most historic institution in Salem. The present edifice is a pretty, domestic-gothic structure, surmounted by two handsome towers. The auditorium and pastor's study are on the second floor, and underneath is John P. Peabody's great fancy goods and furnishing store, one of the most extensive in Essex county, a jewelry store and the Exchange bank. Here was erected the first church building in Salem, about 1634, and here on this spot has generation after generation worshipped in four successive edifices. Here, on July 20, 1629, and Aug. 6, of the same year, was formed the first independent church organization in the new world. Other church organizations existed in America prior to this, but they were all effected in the old world. The history of the First church at Salem is a part of the history of American civilization. It constitutes the most important chapter in the ecclesiastical history of the new world. On July 20, 1629, Samuel Skelton was chosen pastor, and Francis Higginson, teacher. On Aug. 6, following, deacons and ruling elders were chosen, and the organization completed. Among the succeeding pastors have been Roger Williams, John Higginson, Hugh Peters, Hon. Charles W. Upham, Dr. Briggs, James T. Hewes, and the present minister, Rev. Fielder Israel. For fuller information the reader is referred to an address delivered by Mr. Upham on Dec. 8, 1867, to the chapter in "Old Naumkeag" on the "Settlement of Salem," and the "Sketch of Salem." *East* (Unitarian), Brown street, opposite the common. Rev. Geo. H. Hosmer, pastor. The first branch of the First church, organized in 1718. The front of the present church edifice is very imposing, with its two round towers. The interior is the best specimen of pure gothic architecture to be found in Salem, and one of the very few edifices in this city, public or private, which has any attempt at architectural style. *Tabernacle* (Congregational), corner Washington and Federal streets. Founded in 1735 by an unhappy division in the First church. Rev. Samuel Fiske, the first pastor, seceded from the First with more than half the members. In 1769 the church government became Presbyterian, but resumed Congregationalism in 1784. The present house was built in 1854. Rev. DeWitt S. Clark is pastor. *North* (Unitarian), Essex street, between North and Beckford. Rev. Edmund B. Willson, pastor. A branch of the First, in 1770. The first house of worship stood on the corner of Lynde and North streets, where Judge Lord's house new stands. It was there that young Dr. Barnard, then pastor, on a Sunday morning in 1775, dismissed the congregation that they might go down to North bridge and prevent the progress of Col. Leslie.

St. Peter's (Episcopal), corner Brown and St. Peter streets. Erected in 1733, and first used on June 25, 1734. The fourth church established in Salem. There was Episcopal preaching in Salem as early as 1626, but it was very objectionable to most of the people. As late as 1777 the legislature affixed a penalty of £100 to the "crime" of reading the Episcopal service. The present building is a good specimen of Gothic architecture; built of granite, with a handsome castelated tower. The willow tree, growing in one corner came from the grave of Bonaparte, at St. Helena. Rev. Charles Arey, D. D., is rector.

The *Church of the Immaculate Conception* (Catholic), Walnut street has a fine interior, having been beautifully frescoed in the spring of 1881. The fine tower was erected in the fall of 1880, and the mellow-toned bell first rang on St. Patrick's day, 1881. The first Roman Catholic house of worship was erected in 1820. In 1838 the attendance, which included the Catholics of the adjoining towns, numbered about 150. Salem now has two societies, the other being St. James, on Federal street; and each of the towns has a society. The *South church* on Chestnut street, Rev. E. S. Atwood, has the finest spire in the city, and the *Universalist* on Rust street, Rev. E. C. Bolles, has an artistic interior.

PUBLIC BUILDINGS. *Plummer Hall*, on Essex street, is the seat of the Essex Institute and Salem Athenæum, the most important historical and educational institutions in Essex county. The building occupied by these organizations, was built with a fund of $30,000 bequeathed by Miss Caroline Plummer to the Salem Athenæum. The Institute was formed in 1848 by a union of the Essex County Natural History society with the Essex Historical society. Its objects are general and varied. Perhaps the most important is that of local historical discoveries and the preservation of everything relating to Essex county history, and especially of the towns in this vicinity. The Institute library numbers about thirty thousand bound volumes, and 100,000 pamphlets and volumes of periodicals and newspapers. Every book, manuscript, pamphlet, catalogue, circular, etc., pertaining to local history, finds a welcome here. Also, directories, and state and municipal registers and records, not only in the county, but throughout the world. In addition to the library field, or that of written instruction, the Institute is doing an important work in oral and object education through lectures, concerts, exhibitions and excursions and field meetings. Hours 9 to 1 and 2.30 to 5. The Athenæum is purely a library institution, and contains about 17,000 volumes. The Institute occupies the lower floor and the Athenæum the upper. A small side-room on the first floor contains a rich museum of curiosities from different parts of the world, called the "historical collection." The large natural history collection originally belonging to the Institute, was turned over to the Peabody Academy of science in 1867. It numbered at that time 125,000 specimens. The Institute publishes "The Historical Collections," "The Bulletin," and occasional pamphlets. The libraries of the Essex Agricultural society and of the Southern District Medical society are deposited in Plummer Hall. The main room occupied by the Athenæum library is extremely fine and contains some rare old works of art. In the rear of Plummer Hall is the edifice first occupied by the First church society, built in 1636. Everything connected with these institutions will be shown to the visitor free. The Institute and Athenæum libraries are open from 9 to 1 A. M., 2.30 to 5 P. M. (6 in summer).

Peabody Academy of Science, Essex street, head of St. Peter st. George Peabody gave $140,000 "for the promotion of science and useful knowledge in the county of Essex," naming nine eminent gentlemen as trustees. Of this sum $40,000 was given for the East India Marine hall and the valuable museum of that society. The remainder constitutes a permanent investment. The collections of the Essex Institute and East India Marine society were then united, forming one of the grandest collections in this country. The museum is open free to the public every day (Sundays excepted), and a neat little catalogue will explain what is to be seen and where to find it. Hours from 9 to 12 and 1 to 5.

City Hall, on Washington street, near Essex. Plain, low brick building, with smooth granite front. The city of Salem was incorporated on March 23, 1836, with Leverett Saltonstall as mayor. The first city government was inaugurated in the Tabernacle church. The city hall was first occupied on May 31, 1838. The interior of the hall is equally plain with the exterior, save the Mayor's suite of rooms which is very handsomely furnished, and the aldermanic chamber which is a beautiful room. This room contains a fine portrait of Washington presented by Seth Low; and a small portrait of Mayor Saltonstall. The council chamber contains portraits of Washington and Nathaniel I. Bowditch.

SCHOOL BUILDINGS. The buildings of the State Normal school, and also the Salem high school, and the Oliver primary are on Broad street near Summer. None of them are models of architectural skill or beauty. The Normal school building is a three-story brick structure, well adapted to the purpose for which it is used. This school was established by the Commonwealth in 1854. The city of Salem gave the site and erected the building, receiving from the state therefor, $6000. Richard Edwards and Alpheus Crosby have been principals, and D. B. Hagar, Ph. D., is the present principal. The school is exclusively for females. Salem's school houses do not reflect credit on a

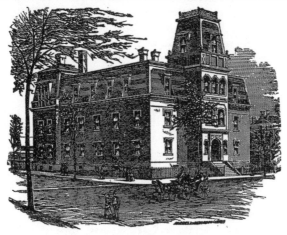

STATE NORMAL SCHOOL.

city of wealth and intelligence, and are universally ill-adapted to educational purposes.

The *Custom House* is on Derby street, at the head of Derby wharf. It is a two-story brick building with ware-house in the rear, and was built in 1819. The Customs collections in Salem are very meagre now, only about $10,000 a year. Formerly they were very large, an immense trade being carried on with foreign ports in all parts of the world. The time was when Salem had the most extensive commerce of any American port. During the quarter ending with Dec., 1807, the duties at this port amounted to $511,000. In those days Derby wharf was lined with merchant vessels from different ports of the old world, sometimes two or three deep. Millions on millions of dollars' worth of goods have been landed here. The old wharf is now fast passing away, the sides crumbling, and warehouses falling.

The *Passenger Station* of the Eastern railway, at the inter-section of Norman and Front streets with Washington, is one of the most imposing buildings in the city. It is built of rough granite, and surmounted on the northerly end with two noble square towers. The freight and passenger traffic of this road at Salem is quite large. The passenger receipts average $150,000 yearly, and the freight $250,000. Branch lines run from here to Marblehead, to Danvers and Lawrence, and to Cape Ann. At the *Northern Depot*, on the other side of the city and at the opposite end of Washington street, trains go to Lowell and Lawrence over the Salem and Lowell, and to Lynnfield, Wakefield and Boston over the South Reading, a branch of the Eastern.

The old *Town House* and market building, in Derby square, is an historic edifice. It was built in 1816, at a cost of $12,000, and was used by the town officials until the City hall was built. The *County Jail* is on St. Peter street. It is a small two-story granite building with jailer's house attached. There are other Essex county jails at Lawrence and Newbury-port.

The *Court Houses*, on Federal street, contain the offices of all the county officials of Essex county, save the registry of deeds for the northern district, which is at Lawrence. There are two buildings. The older one, built in 1841, contains the county offices and the probate court room. The other, built in 1861, is where the supreme judicial and superior courts are held. Sessions of the superior court are also held at Lawrence and Newburyport. Sessions of probate court are held at Salem, Newburyport, Lawrence, and Haverhill. The new court room contains the great portrait of Chief Justice Shaw, by Hunt, the artist's undoubted masterpiece; a smaller portrait of Judge Otis P. Lord of Salem, now on the supreme bench, and a still smaller one of Judge Putnam.

NOTED HOUSES AND PRIVATE RESIDENCES. There are no striking specimens of exterior architecture among Salem houses, although there are many fine old mansions in the town, like the Pickering house on Broad street, built by John Pickering in 1650. It is now owned by one of his descendants, John Pickering. Timothy Pickering, scholar, lawyer, jurist, soldier and statesman was born here. Kernwood, the residence of Mr. S. E. Peabody, is a charming place, as is the estate of Mr. C. A. Ropes in the same section. Judge Endicott's house, No. 365 Essex street, is a fine specimen of the old-time Salem mansion. The residence of Mr. James P. Cook on Bridge street is attractive without and within, and contains a rich collection of works on China, one of the finest in this country. House No. 12 Lynde street, the residence of Hon. Wm. D. Northend, was once the home of Rufus Choate.

The *Hawthorne House*, No. 21 Union street, the house in which the great romance writer was born, should be visited. It is an old-fashioned, two-story gambrel-roof house with a monster chimney in the centre. Hawthorne was born in the northeast corner room, on July 4, 1804. He also lived in a large old house which stood on Herbert street, and now stands in back toward Union street. One of his favorite haunts was the old Ingersoll house at the foot of Turner street, frequently designated *The House of Seven Gables*. It is claimed on the one hand that this house, which has many gables, and in those days had more, suggested to Hawthorne the name of his now famous romance. On the other hand it is alleged that he once said he had no particular house in view. This we can hardly construe literally. The story was given to the world as a local romance. The opening chapter more nearly describes this house than any other in Essex county. We know, too, that Hawthorne passed much of his time there.

HISTORIC LOCALITIES. At *North Bridge*, on North street, the citizens of Salem met Col. Leslie and three hundred British regulars on Feb. 26, 1775. Leslie was after some cannon which were stored in North Salem. He landed in Marblehead and marched to Salem. The citizens met him at North bridge and told him he could not proceed. A compromise was finally effected by which Leslie was allowed to march his men across the bridge and then return to Marblehead and embark for Boston. Thus ended the first armed resistance to England's power, without bloodshed. *Harmony Grove*, in North Salem, is one of the most beautiful cemeteries in this country. It contains sixty-five acres of land, the western portion extending into Peabody. In summer, the cemetery is charming with its flowers and plants and foliage. The gateway, a rustic arch of stone, is worthy of attention, and many of the monuments and pieces of sculpture are very beautiful. George Peabody, the London banker and philanthropist, is buried here. In *Charter street cemetery* were buried Hillard Veren and Martha Corey of witchcraft fame, Richard Derby, Warwick Palfray, Benjamin Lynde, Simon Forrester and Deliverance Parkman, and in the *Broad street cemetery* Sheriff Corwin of Witchcraft fame.

HOTELS. Many years ago Ezekiel Hersey Derby owned nearly all the land in South Salem, it being then unsettled. Here he built a fine summer residence. That residence is now the *Lafayette House*, a most charmingly situated hotel, quiet and secluded. The surroundings are equally attractive. The house is in some respects old-fashioned, but it is that old fashion which we may well wish might never depart—the old fashion of comfort. The Lafayette is on the direct road between Salem and Swampscott, Marblehead and Lynn. Charles F. Kelly is proprietor. The *Farragut House* on Derby Square is another hotel of excellent standing. Mr. James H. Anderson, the proprietor, renovated and refurnished it in 1880, making it one of the neatest "down-town" hotels in the city, and he has placed it on a high plane. The house has a number of fine, large, and elegantly furnished rooms on the second floor, where are also the office, dining hall, and three public parlors, with reading room. The rooms are heated by steam, an especial recommendation to its patrons.

BUSINESS HOUSES. We will note here briefly a few of the many business houses of Salem. There are two monthly, two weekly, two semi-weekly and one daily, papers published: namely, Peabody's Fireside Favorite, Conrad's Pavilion, Observer and Post, Register and Gazette (Mercury, weekly edition), and Daily Evening News. The first two are advertising mediums. The Observer is located on the corner of Essex and Washington streets, where it has been for many years. In the same block is H. P. Ives' bookstore, where may also be found house paper and all kinds of stationery. The Gazette is in the large Hale block. The Register is in the historic Hawthorne building, corner Central and Essex streets, where it has been published many years. The building has been recently remodelled and the lower floor is now occupied by the Shawmut hat store, one of the largest in the county, managed by Geo. H. Smith. The Osbornes occupied this store for some fifty years. Near here, on the corner of Essex and St. Peter streets is located the new and enterprising firm of Merrill & Mackintire, dealers in stationery and room paper. Close by their store is Frank Cousins' dry and fancy goods store, filled with an almost endless variety. It is known as the Beeh-ive. The site occupied by this store was formerly William Gray's garden.

At 198 Essex street is the jewelry store of Geo. A. Collins, who makes a specialty of repairing watches and clocks, and restoring antique articles. In Holyoke building, at the head of the tunnel is J. G. Lowery's fine art store. There is nothing in the matter of fine arts which is not represented here. Mr. Lowery has had many years' experience and is an expert in the business. He also frames all kinds of pictures. His rooms are well worth a visit. In Brown block, next the Observer office, we find C. H. & J. Price, the pharmacists. They have one of the most extensive establishments in Essex county; next door is C. M. Buffum's large hardware store. On the floor above is Dr. A. S. Dudley's dental rooms. The doctor has performed some of the most wonderful pieces of work in the manufacture of artificial palates, noses, and teeth. Hon. W. D. Northend, of the Essex bar, is also located here, and above is Brooks' book bindery. Immediately opposite and under the First church is John P. Peabody's elegant store, where the ladies can find about everything their most fastidious tastes can crave, and even gentlemen can be accommodated in many lines. It is really surprising how any one can put so many articles, and such a variety, in the space which this store occupies. Mr. Peabody has grown into the business from small beginnings, and knows every diverging branch. His store is well worthy to occupy the site of the historic "first church organized in the new world." Speaking more in detail, it is not merely a common dry goods store, but to no small extent a jewelry store, a millinery store, and a ladies' furnishing

goods store. It is such establishments as these that help build
up a small city, because they bring to it business from our
suburban towns.

To any one seeking anything in the furniture line Salem
offers unusual inducements. We find in close proximity, on
Essex street, the two best establishments—the best in Essex
county. At the corner of Barton Square and Essex streets, next
the Barton Square church, are Haskell & Lougee. It is
useless to speak in detail of the place, because everything in
their line of business will be found here. Just beyond, at the
corner of Essex and Crombie streets and near Mechanic Hall,
is the new and commodious store of W. C. Packard & Co.
This store was burned early in 1881 and rebuilt at once, and
reopened on May 4, following. It is now one of the finest
buildings on the street. Here, too, is a full assortment of the
choicest furniture. The old "Ship Tavern," subsequently
known as the Mansion House, occupied the site on Essex
street at the head of Central street, now occupied by the great
dry goods house of Almy, Bigelow & Webber. John Gedney
kept the old tavern in the 17th century; subsequently it was
kept by John Stacey; in 1693 we find it kept by Francis Ellis,
and still later by Henry Sharpe. John Turner built the
Mansion House in 1748, and it was occupied successively by
Judge Andrew Oliver and Capt. Nathaniel West. It was opened
as a public house in 1833, and burned on June 8, 1859. It
was succeeded by the West block, which was enlarged and
remodelled in 1880. The firm of A. B. & W. was estabished
in 1858, and occupied West Block in 1862. The lower floor is
155 feet by 65; the second floor, nearly as large, is occupied
by the same establishment, and also a portion of the third
story. The floors of this store cover an area of one acre.
Goods are manufactured here in the store. The line covers
dry and fancy goods, ladies' and gentlemen's furnishing goods,
dress goods, millinery, carpets, and custom work. James F.
Almy, Walter K. Bigelow, William G. Webber, E. A. Annable,
and C. R Washburn constitute the firm. David Conrad, on
Essex street, near St. Peter street, has one of the finest blocks
in the city since it was rebuilt in 1880. His "Pavilion" ranks
amonk the best stores in the city. Charles A. Ropes, at the

foot of Central street, has probably the largest grain and hay store in Essex county. On North street, at No. 8, F. A. Wendell has one of the best plumbing establishments in the city. Richardson & Waters, on Essex street, near the market, are hardware dealers of experience.

SALEM NECK.

JUNIPER POINT.— WINTER ISLAND.— THE WILLOWS.— A PLEASANT SEA-SHORE SETTLEMENT.

The growth of Salem Neck is somewhat phenominal. Ten years ago the greater portion of the land was used as a pasture, although there were a few small summer cottages, and under the Willows a few children played. Seven or eight years ago several Lowell people came over here from Marblehead, where they had previously summered, and built some small cottages. In 1873, 4 and 5, the number of summer sojourners increased, and during the latter year Mr. Daniel B. Gardner, of Salem, purchased that section then known as the Allen farm, containing about 42 acres, and laid out lots and streets. During the past six years, he has been unremitting in his efforts to improve the "Juniper" settlement, beautifying it with trees and fountains. Water, gas and the indispensable telephone are in place. This settlement contains about 100 houses, and in July and August the population numbers nearly 800 people. In 1880, Mr. Gardner opened a branch grocery store for the accommodation of residents, while butchers, bakers, ice-men, milk-men and all the attendants of city life are to be found. The locality is healthy, pleasant and comfortable. The ocean in front, and a salt water cove in the rear, purify the atmosphere and temper the air. Across the cove is Winter island. This island is the property of the Plummer farm school,

2

Willow Park Pavilion,

SALEM NECK.

MESSRS. DAVIS & FAY of the Essex House, Salem, have leased this house for the season. This is the pleasantest resort in this section. The **Spacious Dancing Hall** will be open afternoon and evening. The Restaurant will be provided with the best the market affords.

ESSEX HOUSE,

SALEM, MASS.

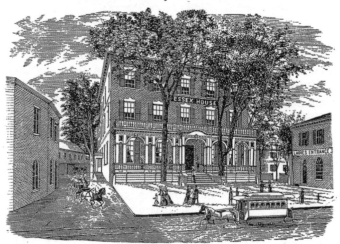

Everything First-class.

Horse Cars for Peabody and Beverly pass the door.

RATES—$2 TO $3 PER DAY.

DAVIS & FAY.

save a small section belonging to the general government for light-house purposes, and the ruins of old Fort Pickering. The frigate Essex, one of the most historic ships of the American navy, was built here in 1799.

The "Willows" section of the Neck, is, perhaps the more historical. Felt says that Salem Neck was occupied by fishermen as early as 1637, at the "point of rocks" on the present Rowell farm near the Rowell homestead. The Hawthornes owned land here at one time. On the left is the Salem city farm, extending along the shore to the Willows. The Almshouse, a large brick building, erected in 1815, stands at the extremity of a lane leading off the main street to the left. A little further along on the main avenue, and near the top of the hill, is a building used as a public pest-house in case of epidemic. Just beyond, on the brow of the hill, stands Fort Lee, now dismantled and crumbling away. A fort was built here as early as 1699, and has existed in one condition and another down to the present time. In 1775 Gen. Henry Lee rebuilt it and mounted guns on it. Hence the name. After the war of the revolution and the war of 1812–14 it was abandoned by the general government. It was again rebuilt during the fratricidal strife of 1861–5. The "Willows" through the liberality of the city and the enterprise of the Naumkeag street railway company has been admirably adapted to the public wants. Here are seats, booths, pavilions, fountains and paths to make pleasant the afternoon. There are some half dozen little dining places on the public grounds where fish dinners or lunches can be had at most reasonable prices. There are none of the swindling prices so often charged at the sea-shore. Steamers often make trips down the harbor and pleasure boats are always to be had. Time was when this locality was a mere waste without a building on it. The only path leading here was a rough and crooked lane. Now all is changed. A broad highway and a line of street cars make the journey short and pleasant, either on foot, or in a private carriage or public conveyance. All this has been done in the face of unexplainable opposition on the part of some citizens and members of the past city governments. As an event of a somewhat remarkable nature in this connection, and as showing how some men

are so constituted that they dislike to see any improvements,
either because the idea did not originate in their barren minds
or because they would seek cheap glory as (penny-wise and
pound foolish) economists, it is due to history to record that a
Salem councilman, in the spring of 1879, would not favor an
appropriation for shade trees at the Neck unless it provided for
closing the restaurants at 8 P. M., and prohibited the band
from playing in the evening. Of course such obstruction as
this could not effect much, though,—

> ".Its proper sphere to hurt, each creature feels,
> Bulls aim their horns, and asses kick their heels."

And, to-day, the land which, in 1873, was taxed for $9800, is
assessed for more than $100,000. The Naumkeag street rail-
way company has made vast improvements at the Willows
during the past two years. In 1879, this company erected a
large and handsome pavilion at the terminus of its track.

DRIVES AROUND SALEM.

To Wenham and Hamilton.— Chebacco.— Suntaug
Lake.— The Danvers Asylum.—Spring Mansion.—
Swampscott and Nahant.—Marblehead.

The roads in the vicinity of Salem present unusual attractions for carriage driving, that between Salem and Gloucester
being unsurpassed by any in New England. It will be found
fully outlined further on, and, therefore, need not be described
here. Another pleasant drive is made through Beverly, Wenham, Hamilton and Ipswich. Crossing Beverly bridge, turn
to the left on to Rantoul street, shortly after entering the
town, which follow to the railroad crossing. Here take the
road leading to the reservoir and Salem water works, which is
open until 6 P. M. The gate leading to the reservoir itself is

open afternoons. This reservoir is 400 feet square and holds 20,000,000 gallons. The road continues to the highway and thence to the pumping station on the shore of Wenham lake, from which Salem and Beverly obtain their water supply. The lake covers an area of 320 acres and contains the purest water to be found in the Commonwealth. The works were set in motion on Dec. 25, 1868. Returning to the public road, we continue along the side of the lake to Wenham village, one of the purest types of a New England village in existence. The town of Wenham was the first of the several towns to be detached from ancient Naumkeag. Hugh Peters preached here in 1636. At the church two roads diverge: That to the left leads to Asbury Grove, the Methodist camp ground, and that to the right through the main street of the village. Both will ultimately lead us to the railway station, from whence we may go to Hamilton village and Ipswich. A branch railway runs from here to Essex. There is some charming rural scenery between here and Ipswich. The camp-meeting ground, mentioned above, contains some three hundred residences and thirty society tents, and in summer has a population varying from five hundred to two thousand during camp-meeting week. Between Wenham depot and Hamilton village we pass the residence of Miss Abigail Dodge ("Gail Hamilton"). It is the old Dodge homestead, and stands back some distance from the street on the left, just before entering the village. One may go from here to Ipswich along a road lined with thrifty-looking farm buildings, or keep to the right and visit Chebacco lakes.

This secluded spot is certainly one of the most delightful on the North Shore. A retired, quiet nook in the woods, approached by a charming shaded driveway leading to a group of as lovely sheets of water as ever the sun shone on. The fishing and boating is unsurpassed, and the scenery strikingly romantic. At the Chebacco House, Messrs. Whipple and Sons can prepare the best dinners or suppers to be eaten in the country. The spring chicken dinners furnished here have a more than local reputation. The home trip may be made through Beverly back roads or through Manchester woods and up along the Beverly shore. If by the former, the drive will be about twenty miles altogether; if by the latter about seventeen. There is also a new road from the Dustan place in Beverly to Chebacco, back of the lakes. Between Beverly proper and Pride's crossing the "back road" will be found fully equal to the shore road. We shall not give minute directions because it is immaterial which way one drives; instinct will lead in the general direction of Salem, and half the romance is in striking boldly into any of the beautiful forest roads and following their winding course to the end.

Perhaps the best inland drive is to Lynnfield and Suntaug lake. Go up Essex and Boston streets to Peabody, then out Foster street to Washington. The second house from the junction of the streets—the two-story yellow one—is the house in which George Peabody was born on Feb. 18, 1795. A short distance beyond, take the right hand road, which leads through a thriving farming community. The large farm with a handsome white dwelling house is Charles Goodrich's. On the hill beyond is Ship-rock, the largest boulder in the country east of the Mississippi, save one in North Carolina. It is 40 feet by 20, and 30 in height and is owned by the Essex Institute. The large brick house surrounded by a flourishing farm is the Peabody alms-house. A mile or so farther on note the two rows of ash trees on either side of the highway along the Bryant estate; and just beyond, the most charming arch made by a double line of locust trees bordering the Gen. Newhall estate. The road by which we enter South Lynnfield village crosses the Boston and Newburyport turnpike and continues on to Wakefield. Making a sharp turn to the right, on the turnpike, by the old Lynnfield hotel, drive past the charming English villa of David P. Ives; then turning into the grove, by the road to the left, pass the residence of Henry Saltonstall and the Swiss villa of Francis Appleton. These are all summer residences, overlooking the beautiful Suntaug lake (formerly known as Humphrey's pond). They are delightful retreats surrounded by groves, parks and lawns. Just beyond Mr. Appleton's, enter upon the turnpike and return to Locust street, through that to the Lynn road, which follow, along a rough but picturesque country road, to Wyoma, a section of Lynn. Turn to the left, pass the Catholic cemetery (formerly a trotting park), the residence of Mr. John L. Shorey, Brown's pond, on the left, and beyond, on the right, in Peabody, look for the Shillaber homestead. The road to Cedar grove cemetery leads off to the right. To Peabody village by way of Washington street completes the trip.

The state lunatic hospital on Hathorne hill, Danvers, should be visited by all who get as near to it as Salem, because it is a building of gigantic proportions. It can be reached by rail, from the Eastern depot (11.30 A. M., or 12.45 and 3.40 P. M.) or by carriage. It is eight miles distant from Salem. Go through Salem to Danversport. The point of land between the two rivers here was originally a grant to Gov. Endicott, who was probably, the first land-holder in the limits of Danvers. Just to the left of here, on a cross road, is the old *Endicott pear tree*, undoubtedly the oldest cultivated fruit tree in the country. Drive through the pleasant village, turning to the left, by the church, and continue a mile and a half, passing through the Plains village. Here the Peabody institute, another of George Peabody's monuments, may be visited. It is pleasantly located amidst a forest of shrubbery and flowers. Two miles further on is Hathorne hill. The surroundings of the hospital, including the walks, drives, terraces, farm buildings, and everything connected with the institution, are most perfectly arranged. The state owns 197 1-2 acres of land. The extreme elevation of the hill is 257 feet above sea level. The hospital building is of brick, four stories, in the domestic-gothic style of architecture, that meaningless style after which so many of our public edifices are built. It is finished in the most lavish manner and yet for want of some strong distinctive architectural style does not impress the visitor in the remotest degree. It is divided into nine sections, an administration building in the centre, and four wings on either side, each falling back some fifty feet or more. The distance from the two extreme points is 1180 feet. Near here is the stone mansion of J. E. Spring, (built 1880-1) which cost about $80,000, one of the finest in New England. Near the Spring mansion lives John G. Whittier, in a charming retreat just off the highway. From the Asylum return to Salem through Peabody, passing the Parris house of witchcraft fame, the Collins house and other points of minor interest.

Swampscott, Lynn and Nahant may be inclosed in a pleasant drive of twenty miles, including return. Lafayette St. to the Lynn road, Sea View ave., to Hotel Preston, around the hotel, main road to Ocean ave., which follow to the old Phillips' homestead in Swampscott; keep to the left and drive around by the shore, to the Ocean and Lincoln houses, through the village to Ocean ave., Lynn; out of this to Lynn beach and to Nahant; drive entirely around the peninsula and return along the beach road, a most delightful spot, to Lynn again. Take Nahant street to Broad, then to Chatham and by Chatham to Essex, and back to Salem over the Forest river road. Arrange to be between Hotel Preston and Nahant from 5 to 6 P. M., when the avenues are alive with fine turnouts. Another drive, comprising a portion of the above, but much shorter, is to Marblehead village, around through Barnegat to the Salem harbor side. Returning through the town to Devereux station, go to the Neck (elsewhere described). Drive around the Neck and back to the station, then turn to the left, follow Ocean avenue to the Clifton House, and then home through the Hawthorne-lined avenue from Clifton station, the Lynn road and Salem and Marblehead road. This covers a distance of about twelve miles.

These drives may be varied somewhat to suit the taste, and, in fact, one who is not limited as to time and has no special point in view cannot do better than to strike out utterly regardless of any one route and drive wherever inclination shall lead on the spur of the moment. Teams for these drives may be obtained at W. S. Jones' on Front street, near the police station; also at Smith & Manning's on Essex street.

PEABODY.

CHURCHES—SCHOOLHOUSES—OTHER PUBLIC BUILDINGS—
BUSINESS HOUSES—PEABODY INSTITUTE—STATISTICAL.

Among the pleasant and thriving towns in the vicinity of
Salem is Peabody. Turning from Essex street to the right
into Boston street and passing through that portion of Salem
known as Blubber Hollow, so called from the odor of the
blubber used in olden times for stuffing leather, we come to a
large elm tree, known as the "big tree." At its base is a
stone dated " June ye 7, 1707," which is supposed to be the date
when this monarch of the forest was located here. A flowing
drinking fountain for man and beast was placed here in 1880
that furnishes a copious supply of pure water summer and
winter. This formerly marked the limits of Salem on the
right. On the left Salem extended to Lynn line. A few years
ago the lines were changed, and now both sides are Salem, to
near the upper end of the old burying ground on the right.
This is probably the oldest cemetery in the town, and is
noted as the burial place of Eliza Wharton. No directions
are needed by strangers seeking the grave, as a well worn
path leads to the spot. The foot stone and a large part of the
head stone have been carried away in chips by relic-hunters.
What is said to be the the oldest stone in the cemetery stands
nearly facing the entrance under a wild cherry tree and bears
this inscription, "Here lyes ye body of James Gyles aged
about 10 years Decease ye 20 of May, 1689." The fine row of
elm trees that front the cemetery were set out in 1843. The
first house is that of Nathaniel Annable, the village black-
smith, whose anvil still responds to his sturdy blows as it has
from father and son for a century in its present location. On
the opposite side of Main street is the old burial ground of the
Quakers, or Friends, who were largely represented in this town
in olden times. A few of the families still reside in the town.

2*

The large mansion on the hill, in the rear, is the residence of
Gen. Wm. Sutton, whose lands extend as far as the eye can see.

On the left of Main street stands the Wallis schoolhouse, on
Sewall street, built in 1869. It has 11 teachers and 590 pupils. On the right of Main street, the building occupied as a
drug store belongs to the heirs of the late Dr. Joseph Shed, a
prominent member of Jordan Lodge of Masons, and who built
a hall in it for the use of the lodge. This lodge was formed in
the old town of Danvers in 1778, but afterward given up, its
records, charter, &c., being destroyed by fire in 1808. In
September, 1808, another charter was obtained and a new
lodge formed. It has continued ever since, and now has an
elegant hall in the Warren bank building. Passing on up
Main street, by the old Danvers bank on the corner of Holten
street, we come to the junction of Main and Washington
streets, where stands the monument. This marks the spot
from which Capt. Foster marched his men to Lexington, April
19, 1775, when seven of them were killed. It is of Danvers

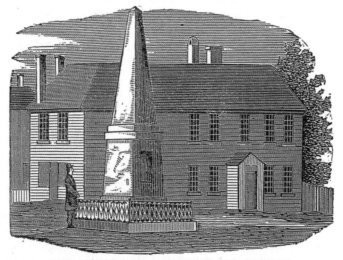

THE MONUMENT AND OLD BELL TAVERN.

granite, 22 feet high, 7 feet square at the base, and was erected
in 1835. The old Bell tavern stood on what is now the lawn
in front of the residence of Hon. A. A. Abbot. In the west

front chamber Eliza Wharton lived and died in 1788. Over the door on the west front was a quaint old sign that read:

> " I'll toll you in if you have need,
> Feed you well and bid you speed."

Over the other door was the sign:

> " Francis Symonds makes and sells
> The best of chocolate also shells."

A short distance up Washington street, stands the Methodist church, organized in 1836. In 1880 a deserted pottery on Washington street was turned into a chapel, and in 1843 this church was purchased of the South Congregational society by the late Timothy Walton, and removed here from the square, the monument being moved to allow it to pass. On the opposite corner is the residence of C. B. Farley, Esq. Above this the residence of J. A. Lord, Esq., formerly that of the late Hon. John W. Proctor. Adjoining this is the harness making establishment of Thomas F. Hutchinson, where may be found a good stock of harness materials, &c. Returning to Main street, the large brick store opposite stands on a portion of the old Southwick estate, noted as being the place where tanning was commenced about 1750. It is occupied by the young and enterprising firm of Bushby & Co., who do a very extensive business in choice family groceries, &c. The handsome residence adjoining is that of Benj. S. Wheeler. A few steps farther and we come to Peabody Institute, founded by the late George Peabody, on June 16, 1852, the one hundredth anniversary of the division of the town from Salem. It was built in 1853-4 of brick, with freestone trimmings, 128x50 feet, and contains a library of 21,000 volumes, and a lecture hall that will accommodate nearly 1000 persons. A full length oil painting of the town's benefactor hangs in the lecture room, with portraits of Rufus Choate and Edward Everett. In the library can be seen an oval miniature of Queen Victoria, presented to Mr. Peabody by her Majesty. It is painted on a plate of solid gold, 14 by 10 inches, and bears the inscription, " Presented to George Peabody, Esq., the benefactor of the poor in London"; also two gold boxes, the Peabody Educational medal, autograph letters and other presents, of which the aggregate value is more than $50,000. Mr. John H. Teague was janitor from 1854 until his decease Dec. 4, 1880. John D. McKean succeeded him. It was from here that the remains of George Peabody were taken to their final resting place on Locust Path in Harmony Grove, on February 8, 1870. He died in London Nov. 4, 1869. In the rear of the Institute is the Eben Dale Sutton Reference library, given to the town by Mrs. Eliza Sutton, whose name will ever be revered by all citizens of Peabody for the beautiful and useful gift. It was opened in June, 1869, and now contains over 1900 volumes of the rarest and most valuable books, free to the use of all. Nearly opposite stands the palatial residence of Mrs. Sutton, with its garden, lawn, fountain, &c. Opposite, on Main street, is one of the best business blocks in the town, known as Sutton block. The upper portion is occupied by Union Post 50, G. A. R., and the lower by stores. The first one is the elegant millinery store of Fernald & Sawyer, who rival the stores of the metropolis with their choice selections of goods. The dry goods store of this firm is also located in this block and is noted throughout the entire section for its wares, and the bargains to be had there. Charles A. Teague, who has the largest and best selected stock of boots, shoes, and gents' furnishing goods in the town, is an occupant of this block. Just above, on the right hand side of Park street, are the elegant grounds and residence of Mrs. J. B. Clement. This house was formerly the parsonage of the Unitarian church, and is now one of the finest in town.

The Unitarian church, next above, was built in 1826. Rev. C. C. Sewall preached here from 1827 to 1841. In 1872 the house was remodelled at an expense of $12,000. In the rear stands the Baptist church, built in 1857, and remodelled in 1865 On the left of Park street, the new residence in process of erection, (May, 1881) is that of Charles A. Teague, the boot and shoe dealer of Sutton block. Returning to Main street the second building on our left is the drug store of D. P. Grosvenor, jr., formerly occupied by the late Sylvester Proctor with whom George Peabody was an apprentice from 1806 to 1810, when he was eleven years of age, and where he laid the foundation of that immense fortune which enabled him to give away over $12,000,000. Mr. Grosvenor is the telegraph operator of the

town, and keeps a well selected stock of goods in his line. He
has some of the old furniture of the store that was probably used by Mr. Peabody. On the opposite side of Main street
stands the neat and handsome church of the Universalist society. This was built in 1832, and the hall then underneath
was used for town meetings before the town of Danvers was
divided. The church has been remodelled several times and is
now second to none in the place.

Warren Bank building is a little farther west, a neat brick
block, occupied by the bank and by the Five Cents Savings bank.
The office of the Peabody Reporter, Thos. McGrath, publisher,
a bright and newsy sheet, is in this building. Above are reading and club rooms, and a Masonic and Odd Fellows hall.
Across the street stands one of the oldest business blocks in
town, known as Allen's building. This was formerly the location of the post office. W. Winslow is located here, with the
largest and finest stock of men's clothing and furnishings in
the town. Baldwin's Hotel, which adjoins this estate, was built
in 1825 by the late Jonathan Dustin and has always been occupied. Washington Simonds kept it for more than 25 years.
W. H. Baldwin is the present landlord and keeps a first
class hotel. In the Square the new Soldier's monument
is to be located in September. It is to be of Hallowell
granite, 50 feet high, surmounted by a statue of America. Its cost will be $6,500. Beyond is the depot of
the Eastern railroad and branches. This stands on a
portion of what was once known as Wallis mill-pond, which
in the writer's youthful days, teemed with fish. Alewives by
the thousands passed through here in the spring, on their way
to Brown's and Spring ponds, where they spawned and returned to the sea. The refuse from the factories and tanneries
fouled the streams so that the fish deserted them years ago.
Opposite stands the South church, formerly the third church
of Salem, gathered on Sept. 23, 1713, and was known as such
till 1759. This is the fourth edifice built on this site, the first
having been torn down in 1836; the next one was dedicated
Feb. 1, 1837, and sold to the Methodists in 1843; another (just
completed) was burned in the great fire of Sept. 22, 1843, when
twenty-one buildings were destroyed; the present structure

was dedicated Aug. 10, 1844, and the church now numbers over three hundred members. In the rear of the church can be seen the town house, built just before the division of the town in 1855. It is a building that the town has outgrown. N. H. Poor, Esq., has held the position of Town Clerk for 20 years, and Selectman for a score of years. It is occupied by town officers and the Peabody high school. The latter was founded in 1850, and now has three teachers and 73 pupils.

Central street was once noted for its potteries, where earthen wares were made, known throughout New England as Danvers China. One only of the potteries is now in operation. The Bowditch school on this street has six teachers and 216 pupils. The high hill in the rear is known as Buxton's hill, the location of the water reservoir is one hundred and fifty-nine feet above tide-water. From its top the flames of burning Charlestown were seen in 1775. This section of the town is noted for its excellent farms, and was where the Danvers yellow onion originated. Returning to the square and up Lowell streets, we pass, at No. 13, the extensive stove and tin ware establishment of D. A. & F. H. Caskin who keep an excellent variety of stoves, furnaces and housekeeping-goods. They also do plumbing and general jobbing in their line. In the old Dustin building just above is the office of the "Peabody Press," Albert Vittum, manager; Charles D. How-ard, editor and proprietor. It is now in its 22nd volume and has a large circulation. In the rear of Lowell street stands the elegant St. John's (catholic) church, a pure gothic structure completed in 1880.

On Lowell street stands the handsome brick building of the fire department, where two steamers, one hose carriage, and ladder truck are kept. Above, opposite, is the plain and un-pretending St. Peter's (Episcopal) church, founded in 1874, built in 1876, and improved in 1881. In the rear of Lowell street is the Center schoolhouse. It has eleven teachers and 560 pupils. This street leads to what is called the "Kingdom," where there are many families of Kings, but no one of them is a ruler. This is also a farming region. Returning to the square we pass Upton's block, which contains stores, offices, post-office, and a dance hall. The homestead of the late Gen.

Gideon Foster, who marched his men to the battle of Lexington, in 1775, from this town, stands on the corner of Main and Foster streets. Foster street is lined with tanneries and currying shops, which do a very large business. Just above its junction with Washington street are the extensive works of the Danvers bleachery, where millions of yards of cloth are bleached and colored annually. The second house above the junction, on the right, is the house in which George Peabody was born. Beyond is South Peabody, where are a number of granite quarries and extensive farms. Cedar Grove Cemetery is located here. It is 133 acres in extent, and was laid out in 1859. In the suburbs of the town are four smaller schools with 4 teachers and 117 pupils, making a total of 22 schools, with 5 male and 38 female teachers, and 1669 pupils. The town expends about $22,700 for schools annually. Its valuation is $6,311,050, and its area is 9,050 acres; has 1340 dwellings, 121 steam boilers with 4554 horse power; 718 horses, 523 cows, and a population of about 9080 souls. The original town of Danvers was incorporated in 1757. The town was divided into Danvers and South Danvers in 1855. The name of South Danvers was changed to Peabody in 1868.

BEVERLY.

Its History.—Description of the Sea Shore Section.— Pride's Crossing, Beverly Farms.—Rapid Development of the Shore Section.

Across an arm of the sea from Salem, where the North river joins Beverly harbor, is the town of Beverly. The bridge here is 1484 feet in length and was built in 1788-9. The Wenham water pipe rests on piles on the westerly side. Beverly is one of the oldest settlements in the Commonwealth. It formed a part of Salem until 1668, when it was incorporated as an inde-

pendent town. John and William Woodbury and Roger Conant were among the first settlers. The first meeting house
was built about 1656, with Rev. John Hale as pastor, Hon.
John P. Hale, Hon. Nathan Hale and Rev. E. E. Hale are
numbered among his direct descendants. A second church
was established at North Beverly in 1713, with Rev. John
Chipman as pastor. He married a daughter of Rev. John Hale.
Chief Justice Gray is of their descendants. Agriculture is a
pursuit of considerable importance, especially at Ryall's Side,
Centerville and North Beverly. In the last named section is
the noted Cherry Hill farm of R. P. Waters, and also the extensive and picturesque estate by Wenham lake which John
C. Phillips is making into one of the most beautiful in the
country. The manufacture of boots and shoes is now the
leading industry of the town. The value of the products of
these shops cannot be less than two millions annually, and
they employ about 1500 persons.

Few towns in Massachusetts have made such rapid strides in
the onward march of progress during the last sixteen years.
The water supply and fire apparatus, and the streets and public
buildings are on a metropolitan scale almost. The Wenham
lake water pipes penetrate every section of the town; the fire
department houses are in good condition and equipped with
superior apparatus; the roads are usually among the best in
the county. It is true that these things cost much money,
and the town has a large debt, but the last few years have de-
monstrated the wisdom and foresight of all the expenditure.
The finest public building in the town is Odd Fellows hall on
Cabot street, corner of Broadway. It is a handsome brick
building and has one of the richest lodge rooms in the country.
The architecture of the room borders on the Grecian; the walls
and ceiling are richly and elaborately frescoed, and eight oil
paintings enliven the four sides. The carpets and furniture
and lodge paraphernalia are exquisite. The town building nearly opposite is commodious, and contains beside the usual offices
two good halls and a public library of 5000 volumes. The
Briscoe school building near the common is another handsome
edifice. The Masonic block corner of Cabot and Washington
streets, built in 1867, at a cost of $20,000, contains the post

office and national and savings banks. Among the fine residences in the village are those of Hon. John I. Baker on Abbott street, Hon. Francis Norwood on Cabot street, Capt. Newman on Lathrop street and Dr. Haddock on Bartlett street. Dr. H. has a delightful place, his flower garden being one of the richest in the town. In his house are some rare and curious objects, the most interesting of which is the old clock of which we present a picture. It was brought from Amsterdam about 1663 by Capt. Foster. It came into the doctor's hands some years ago in a dilapidated condition. He entrusted it to Mr. George A. Collins, the jeweler in Salem, who restored it to its present beautiful and artistic condition. Robert Rantoul, the great statesman and scholar stands at the head of

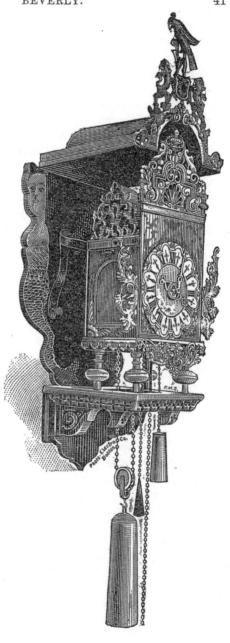

Beverly's distinguished men. Graduating at Harvard in 1826, he practised law in Essex county, was representative to the general court, collector of the port of Boston, United States district attorney, succeeded Daniel Webster in the United States senate, and finally died, while a member of the national house of representatives. Contemporary with Rantoul was Isaac Ray, a distinguished writer on medical jurisprudence and mental disease; Wilson Flagg, the great naturalist; also, Rev. A. P. Peabody, an eminent divine, now connected with Harvard, and Hon. Nathan Dane. Beverly has a population of about 8500. According to the census of 1875 it contained 1,399 dwellings. The amount of capital invested in manufactures was (1875) $314,700. The fishing business has diminished largely. The value of the cod brought to its ports in 1875 was $131,000. The valuation of the town in 1878 was $5,386,600 real estate; and $2,372,300 personal; polls, 1,910; rate of taxation, $14.80, per $1,000. The art connoisseurs who visit Cape Ann will find in Beverly one of the most attractive institutions that the county affords, in the works of the "Beverly pottery." Here they will see accurate reproductions of all the best specimens of ancient pottery, literal copies of some of the finest pieces now in the old world art museums. Beverly has always had excellent deposits of clay within her borders, and besides the early brick manufactory, was among the earliest to establish manufactories of pottery here in this country. Of early workers as early at least as 1700 were members of the Balch and Hayward families, the latter of whom owned land immediately contiguous to the present Beverly pottery, if they did not include that, and there were traces of their work in that vicinity when the present pottery grounds were graded thirteen years ago. The Kettle family also had cunning workers in clay here in the early days and those skilled in the art emigrated hence to Charlestown, Mass., Exeter N. H. and elsewhere. This work has always been more or less prosecuted here ever since; Tarbell's ware being well known as a Beverly product for many years; Mr. Jesse Dodge who died a few years since, being the last survivor of those who worked at Tarbell's pottery. Mr. Charles A. Lawrence established the present Beverly pottery in continuation of those previously here, and has worked out great improvements in this kind of work in many convenient and curious devices, attaining a large sale, and many visitors come to see and purchase the curious specimens of clay handiwork there made.

The Beverly shore is a section of unsurpassed attractions to those who love rural scenery; especially lovely is it when viewed from the harbor at a short distance from shore. Rocky bluffs, beaches, and coves are pleasingly blended; trees of bountiful and beautiful foliage crown the hill crests in the rear, while here and there we spy the red roof of some summer dwelling—here, perhaps, a pretty Swiss villa in the centre of a broad lawn and surrounded with luxuriant flower beds; there a stately mansion overlooking the sea; and anon a Norman or Queen Anne villa crowning some summit and frowning over all its neighbors. The little hastily built sea side cottage, costing from $600 to $1000, has given way to the extensive establishment costing from $10,000 to $25,000. Hale street, which branches off from Cabot near the South church, is the main thoroughfare along this shore, and extends to Manchester, a distance of seven miles—some times at the water's edge and again a half mile from the extreme end of some point. Or we may turn from Cabot street into Washington, and from that into Lathrop. The house on this latter corner is the old Rantoul mansion. It has sometimes been occupied by Rev. A. P. Putnam of Brooklyn. Next beyond, on Lathrop street, is the English villa of Wm. M. Whitney, with a broad lawn in front and a forest of shrubbery in the rear and on either side. At the top of the little hill across the valley, we come to Hale street and turn to the right. The cottage in the little grove on the knoll is Israel Whitney's. And now we keep to the right and follow Ober street, past Charles Elliott's pleasantly located estate on the hill overlooking the harbor and surrounding towns, and the beautiful new cottage house of Wm. F. Ashton of Salem, built in 1881. On the same side of the street, a little further along and surrounded by an imposing granite wall, are the extensive grounds and mansion of B. F. Burgess. This estate extends back from the water about a quarter of a mile and is one of the finest on the coast. Adjoining the

Burgess estate on the same side is William Sohier's residence, and also the Bardwell estate. Opposite Mr. Burgess's and next beyond the Bardwell estate is the fine residence of Alexander S. Porter; and next is that of Mrs. Rodgers. Across the cove on the next point of land is Hospital point lighthouse, reached by a new street leading off Neptune street. The elegant mansion next to the lighthouse belongs to Amory A. Lawrence of Boston. It is in the picturesque Queen Anne style. In close proximity, is Henry W. Peabody's new residence—both built in 1881.

As we return to Hale street along Neptune, we pass on the right at the bend of the way the M. W. Shepard estate, occupied by Joseph W. Lefavour of Salem. Beyond it, approached by a private way is Wm. D. Pickman's new and magnificent mansion (built 1881), in some respects unequalled. It is after the pattern of the Salem houses of 1750 to 1800. Nearer to Hale street is Mrs. Willard Peele's residence. These estates are enclosed with a castellated granite wall, while on the opposite side of the street, enclosed by a like wall, is a large park belonging to them. In the woods, some distance back may be seen the massive granite mansion of Andrew K. Ober, overlooking the ocean and surrounded by beautiful groves. Brackenberry lane leads to Patch's beach and the residence of Mrs. David Sears. Prince street leads to the summer residences of John G. Cushing (on Cushing point), Richard T. Parker, Mrs. John B. Silsbee and S. Endicott Peabody. Across the cove from this point is another frowning stone mansion, a castle almost, that of Mrs. Franklin Dexter. It looks from the water very much like a small Rhinish castle. If now we return to Hale street and continue along it we shall pass through a charming wooded park. The estates on the right are those of Mrs. Dexter and John G. King, both hidden from view. Those on the left are George Z. Silsbee, W. G. Saltonstall, Mrs. Geo. H. Shaw, Waldo Higginson and J. P. Gardner's heirs. Next on the right beyond the beach is the fine large mansion of Mrs. J. S. Cabot. Directly opposite, a little distance from the street, is the Swiss villa of Hon. Martin Brimmer. The cottage next beyond Mrs. Cabot's, on the same side, and partially hidden in *arbor vitæ* is C. U. Cotting's and close to it is that of

G. A. Goddard. Some distance in from the street, beyond these, is Mr. A. Cochrane's, built in 1881, and near it a new house built by C. G. Loring. On the hill opposite Mr. Cotting are Wm. Endicott, Jr., and Sidney Bartlett. Still further along, on the very brow of the hill, is Francis W. Palfrey's Swiss villa, and next that of Francis Bartlett. On Thistle street, beyond Mr. Bartlett's, is the residence of Gen. C. L. Peirson, back of which is a new experimental farming establishment of Augustus P. Loring, and between that and Pride's crossing the sightly estate of James F. Curtis. The driveway to the right, just before we reach the Pride's crossing station, leads to Plum Cove beach and the estates of C. W. Loring, C. G. Loring and the villa of P. T. Jackson.

If, just beyond the station, we turn down the road to the right, we shall visit a cluster of summer mansions most charmingly situated, amid parks, groves, gardens and lawns, where the foliage is luxuriant and the air filled with the perfume of liberal acres of flowers, and where nature has been assisted in the beautifying process by all that art can suggest and wealth supply. Here are natural and artificial forests, meadows, and fields of grain and grass, interspersed with ponds, rivulets, carriage roads, bridle paths and foot paths. The new house on the left, built in 1881, belongs to John T. Morse, Jr.; next is the cottage which he occupies, then those of E. Rollin Morse, and John T. Morse, Sen. The house on the right nearly opposite the last named is Mrs. Judge B. F. Thomas. The old fashioned mansion in the hollow beyond belongs to F. Gordon Dexter. Back of this road, on our right as we enter, is another series of houses. Beginning next to the Lorings there are, in order, George Gardner, Wm. C. Paine and S. B. Schlessinger on the immediate shore, Miss Paine, and F. L. Higginson behind these. Continuing to the beach and coming out at Beverly Farms we pass, on the way, the estates of Franklin Haven, T. A. Neal, R. S. Rantoul and Mrs. S. Cabot. Few of these houses can be seen from Hale street or from the railway. Beyond the station, the white brick house belongs to Jonathan Preston and the yellow one to Mrs. E. A. Boardman.

The beautifully situated mansion on the point towards Manchester-by-the-Sea belongs to Col. Henry Lee. This Beverly

Farms section is so called because it was once comprised in two great farms. John Blackleach originally owned a farm which extended from Mr. Haven's present residence to Manchester-by-the-sea. He sold to John West, and he in turn to his son Thomas. Mary West, a daughter of the latter, married Robert Woodbury and thus the farm was divided. Woodbury built the house now occupied by Dr. Curtis and which bears date 1673. The other farm was owned by William Woodbury and extended in the other direction to Patch's beach. The unique Swiss villa seen from Beverly Farms in the distance on a "back" street belongs to Mrs. Ozias Goodwin, and near it is W. B. Sewall's cottage. Others in this vicinity are owned F. S. Morrison, Charles Storrow, Henry Dexter, Henry Adams, Mr.'Luke, and Mrs. Parkman, while further along the shore toward Manchester-by-the-Sea, is Mr. S. T. Morse's elegant villa. And on the highlands opposite, are the prominent and equally pleasant estates of C. H. Dalton, J. Elliot Cabot, Dr. R. W. Hooper, and Thornton K. Lothrop.

We have now completed our tour of the sea-shore section of Beverly, and seen how wonderfully changed it is from what it must have been twenty years ago. Men now living remember when the entire sea-shore section of the town was assessed for $25,000; to-day the non-residents alone are assessed at for least *one and a half millions* of dollars on real estate. A telephone is much needed in this section, but for some reason the town authorities will not grant permission for its construction.

MANCHESTER-BY-THE-SEA.

This is one of the oldest, as it is one of the most charming
of the North Shore resorts. Its four miles of coast is a pleas-
ing combination of bold headlands, pretty beaches and quiet
coves. During a storm one may behold gigantic seas dashing
against the projecting bluffs with sufficient force to make the
granite walls tremble, while boats ride quietly at anchor in the
coves; and in pleasant weather the waves roll gently up the
beaches and break noiselessly on the rocks. The air of Manchester-by-the-Sea is tonic, and a spirit of freshness and vigor
pervades every one who inhabits its shores. A well-known
ex-mayor of Cambridge comes here as soon as the snow is off
the ground and remains until the return of cold weather,
because it is the only place where he can get relief from Asthma
and hay-fever.

The town of Manchester originally formed a part of ancient
Salem, from which it was detached on May 14, 1645, being the
next after Wenham, and incorporated as an independent
municipality. The early name was Jeffrey's Creek, so called
from William Jeffrey, the first settler. It was once a fishing
port of some note, but that industry has practically disap-
peared. Some of its people engaged extensively in the manufacture of furniture, but with the depression of 1873-9, the
business declined to a minimum. It is recovering somewhat
of late. The valuation of the town is about two and a half
millions, and the rate of taxation in 1881 about $5 per $1000.
The population in 1880 was 1640, and the area of the town
4310 acres. The principal settlement is at the head of the cove
on Jeffrey creek. Here are three churches, Baptist, Orthodox
and Methodist—stores, schools, halls and the like. A good
hotel is wanting. About a third of a mile from the village is
the only hotel in this part of the town, the Masconomo. It is

one of the finest sea-shore caravansaries on the coast and was
built by Junius B. Booth in 1878 and opened to the public in
June of that year. Without and within it is a model of hotel
architecture. When Mr. Booth built his villa, which now
forms an annex to the hotel, he selected the finest site on the
Manchester shore, and every guest at the Masconomo has the
benefit of that judicious selection. In general outline and
interior finish it reminds us of one of those fascinating hotels
on the shores of the Swiss lakes or among the snowy Alps.
On the northern front is a garden and park, beyond which the
hill falls away to the cove and the village. On the southerly
side broad lawns slope to the beach. This beach is known as
Singing beach, because of the peculiar musical sound of the
sand when struck with the foot or by an incoming wave. The
New York Graphic says that, in selecting this spot, Mr. Booth
studied the coast very thoroughly from Long Branch to Old
Orchard. Those who follow him in the study and make up
their conclusions at his hotel will speedily assent to the claim
that he holds the gem of the North Atlantic sea coast. Mr.
Booth's estate is a superb lawn of twelve acres looking out on
a smooth, broad crescent of shore, whose sand, by some pecu-
liarity of its particles, actually whistles as you tread upon it.
Beaten hard by the surf, it is compact and almost unyielding to
tread or wheel, and sloping gently, has a splendid floor for the
bather, with no perils from undertow, the reefs, far outside,
receiving the first force of the sea. By the trend of the shore
line the beach fronts almost due south, and the dreaded northeast wind comes to the Masconomo house across eight miles of
pine woods. The hotel was named for the Indian chief,
Masconomo. Its front is 240 feet, depth 52 feet, and height
three stories. Within are a dining room 77 feet by 32, hotel
and telegraph offices, parlors and twenty-two guests' rooms on
the first floor; twenty-four rooms for guests on the second floor,
and thirty on the third. The octagon hall in the centre of the
house contains four large fireplaces which throw out cheer and
warmth on stormy nights when "the ocean roars up the beach"
and the "gusty blast mingles with our speech." The building
is surmounted with a tower which rises 70 feet above sea level.
An annex on the westerly end, built in 1880, contains billiard

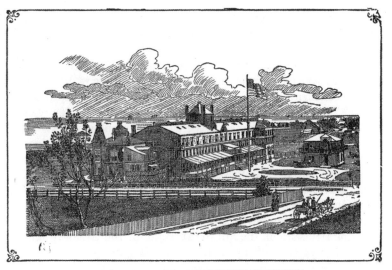

MASCONOMO HOUSE, MANCHESTER-BY-THE-SEA.

hall, bowling alley and sleeping rooms. The whole institution
is lighted with gas. Connected with it is a stable with horses
and carriages.

Some of the best drives of Essex county radiate from here.
One may ride or walk for miles along the pathways of costly
estates or turning inland drive through pleasant valleys, inside
fertile farms or in the "deep solitude" of the forest. The road
to Essex through the noted Essex woods is peculiarly pleasant
and romantic on a summer afternoon or in the early morning.
As we enter the town from Beverly we note first, on the right
and some distance from the road, the residence of Benj. G.
Boardman. Near it is that of his son, Commodore T. Dennie
Boardman. The cottage on the point of rocks near West
Manchester station is also owned by the former. The peculiar
looking structure on the hill to the right of the highway and
to the left of the railway is Henry L Higginson's new residence. He has been several years building it and has expended thousands of dollars on it. On the further side of the hill
is a road leading to West Manchester depot and a cluster of
summer cottages. Among them are those of N. B. Mansfield,
Dr. Bartol and W. C. Cabot. Dr. Bartol's is the cottage with
the tower on top, and near it is his observatory. West Manchester is a remarkably cool place. Evenings, when the heat
in Salem or Boston is almost unendurable, a summer overcoat
will be needed here.

Pursuing our way to the village we pass the town house and
Congregational church; turning to the right, follow railroad
avenue across the railway and up the hill to the Masconomo.
The large, prominently located residence on the hill to the left
was occupied during several years by M. B. Conway, the actor.
The red-roofed cottage on the top of the hill, a little further up,
on Thunderbolt-rock, was for many years the summer residence
of the late James T. Fields. At the Masconomo we turn to
the right and drive along the old Neck road a few rods and
then take the driveway to the right. The white farm house
on the right belongs to the Smith estate. The fine establishment on the left, fronting on the Neck road, with the
grove in the rear (formerly the Martin estate) is occupied by
David B. Kimball of Salem. Ascending the hill on the Neck

we have the old O. S. Fowler place on the right and two fine
residences on the left owned by Hon. J. Warren Merrill, the
further one occupied by Mr. Sawyer (built 1880) and the other
built in 1881. The house on the top of the hill, with pointed
tower, is the residence which Mr. Merrill occupies himself;
just below it is E. E. Rice's cottage. A driveway encircles the
Neck and the visitor should go around on the westerly side
and return on the easterly. The first house which confronts
us as we ascend the hill at the further end is that of George B.
Howes of Boston (built 1880) one of the most costly on the
coast,—about $30,000 having been expended here. Adjoining
it is Gen. A. P. Rockwell's (built 1880–81). These houses are
nearly a hundred feet above the level of the sea. From the
brow of the hill as we return, may be had a fine view of the
ocean, bay, harbor and town. We return from the Neck by a
road which passes between a little fresh-water pond and Lob-
ster cove. The point of land on the right, across the cove, is a
part of the Hemenway estate, now occupied by Lewis Cabot.
The next estate along this road on the same side is that
of Russell Sturgis, jr., and adjoining that is Mrs. Jedediah
Cobb's residence. This brings us back to the Masconomo.

The street which leads from the depot to the Masconomo
continues across the old Neck road past the hotel to Singing
beach. Another street branches off the Neck road just beyond
the hotel, and we follow it past Mr. Gilbert's residence, the
last on the left before entering the grove; and Mrs Stephen H.
Bullard's, the last on the right. It terminates at the charming
English villa of Mrs. John H. Towne of Philadelphia. The
visit to Mrs. Towne's should by all means include Eagle-head,
that grandest old headland of Massachusetts bay. Leaving the
carriage we walk down any of the embowered paths leading to
the base of the ledge and then clamber up its steep side until
we are on a level with the tops of the trees and one hundred
and thirty feet above the sea, which breaks along the cragged
rocks at our feet. Now it rolls softly, almost noiselessly up
the side of some sloping ledge, and anon dashes against a perpendicular front. The white winged craft which sail to and
fro below us, as we sit here, look like toy ships. This on a
lovely May afternoon. How changed the scene on a dark

winter's night when a south-easterly storm rages. The damp
snow which half blinds us makes the distance to the water
seem double what it really is.   The wild waves bear down on
our post like an army attacking a fort, as if, in their wild rush,
they fain would carry all before them. As they approach
nearer, rolling now like mountains, they seem to pause for a
moment as if for renewed breath, and then to throw themselves against the giant rock in a perfect rage. Above the
beating of the storm, above the howling of the forest trees as
they bend before the wind, rises the roar of this furious war of
the waters and the rocks, like ten thousand infuriated demons,
each bent on destroying the other and ruling both land and
sea. It is difficult at such a time to believe the sea inanimate.

If now we return to the main road through the village, we
may continue on towards Gloucester. The large, old-fashioned
house some distance to the right which we see, about the time
we cross the railway after leaving the village, is the Dana
house, the first summer residence built in Manchester. During
many years, and until his death in 1878, it was the summer
home of Hon. Richard H. Dana, the scholar and poet, the
friend, companion and contemporary of the poet Bryant, and
the contemporary of Caleb Cushing. The fine estates of
Greely S. Curtis and Mrs. Emily F. Curtis are near the Dana
place, but hidden from our sight by the woods. The drive
through this wood for about a mile is undoubtedly the most
charming between Salem and Gloucester. The settlement just
beyond the woods is known as Kettle Cove. There are a few
farms here and some fishermen's houses; also two or three
summer cottages. The estate of T. Jefferson Coolidge lies off
to the right across the cove on a point of land. In close proximity is Rev. James Freeman Clark's estate, one of the newer
ones.

The Crescent Beach House, at Kettle Cove, was built in 1873,
and has been enlarged until now it will accommodate 150
guests. It was kept by Mr. Allen Knowlton for many years,
but has now been taken by Mr. W. P. Davis of Gloucester who
has had a life experience in hotels at the North and in Florida.
He will maintain the same high standard which has made this
place so popular in the past. This house has a superior loca-

tion, a fine house, and provides a first-class table, leaving
nothing to be desired by the guests. It is sheltered from the
north and east winds by the dense woods, a short distance
inland. In the cove the opportunities for boating and bathing
are excellent. Some marked improvements have been made
during the past season.

MAGNOLIA.

THE NEWEST SUMMER RESORT — ITS RAPID GROWTH — HOTELS AND PRIVATE RESIDENCES—NORMAN'S WOE.

Magnolia is the newest summer resort on the North Shore.
Its growth has been something surprising upon first thought,
but when we fully realize its varied attractions, we shall only
be surprised that it was not earlier settled by some of the
seekers for sea-shore summer homes. The place is reached by
a road turning to the right off the Salem and Gloucester road,
just beyond the Crescent Beach House, or by a road which turns
off at this house. The first real summer residence was built
here in 1872, by Charles E. Billings, W. O. Trowbridge, J. S.
Potter and Lucien Chase, of Newton. The second was built
by Mr. Goodwin in 1873, since when each year has added to
the number until there are now some thirty cottages, many of
which are unusually fine, and also several hotels, stables,
stores, etc. To Mr. Allen Knowlton is due the credit of start-
ing Magnolia on the road to prosperity. He built the Crescent
Beach House some years ago, opened a barge line from
Manchester and finally secured the Magnolia railroad station.
The next man to become interested in the place was Daniel W.
Fuller, of Swampscott, who purchased all the land on the
"point" in 1867. Much of this he sold in building lots. He
also erected several cottages of his own, and in 1877 he built
the westerly wing of the Hesperus House. In 1879 he added
the easterly wing and the pagoda between, and otherwise
improved the surroundings. The Hesperus will now accom-

modate about a hundred guests. It commands a magnificent
view of the ocean and the North Shore, and the rooms are
mostly large, bright and airy. It will long remain a monument
to Mr. Fuller's industry and good taste. He did not live to see
the fulfilment of his high anticipations as to the future of
Magnolia. He was killed by falling down the shaft of a mine
at Leadville, Col., on Feb. 19, 1880. His death was a sad blow
to a large circle of friends, and a serious loss to the little
community of which he was the leading spirit. There are,
besides the Hesperus, four good hotels at Magnolia point.
They are Willow cottage, Oceanside, Oak Grove and Sea View.
Mrs. Fuller will continue to manage the Hesperus, with the
assistance of Theophilus Herrick, formerly of the Marlboro,
Boston. She has very much improved the house since the last
season by additions and changes.

The Ocean-Side, as its name truly indicates, is near a very
picturesque shore, having a fine elevation; views from the
rooms and the extensive piazzas, of fields, woods, islands, the
bay and the broad ocean are most excellent. Mrs. O. Paige
kept this house last year, receiving much praise for its neat-
ness and order and particularly for the excellence of the table.
She continues the management this year and with increased
conveniences will doubtless win new laurels. The guests of last
season with few exceptions have engaged rooms the present year.
Willow Cottage, near the Hesperus, is the oldest established
hotel here and one the reputation of which is too well known
to require any words of praise from this source. Mr. and
Mrs. Bray, who will manage it during the season of 1881, also
have the use of Norman cottage which adjoins it. A row of
graceful willows in front of the cottage gives name to it and
adds to its attractiveness. *The Sea View House* is near the
above named hotel and once formed an annex to it. Mrs. M.
C. Honnors is the proprietress in 1881 as in 1880, and past
management is a guarantee of what the future will be. Mrs.
Honnors has had the house put in fine order throughout. It will
comfortably accommodate twenty-five guests. Some two hundred feet back from the old Magnolia point road stands the
Oak Grove House, a most delightfully situated hotel. A
very handsome grove of oaks in the rear is much admired by

all guests; and not less the pretty lawn in front. This cottage has room for fifty guests. The cottage is of that size which enables the proprietress, Mrs. R. C. Hunt, to have a personal supervision of the wants of her guests.

The Salem Cadets encamp on the hill here some time during the month of August in each year, and their band discourses music for the benefit of all the residents. Magnolia is, beyond question, in some respects, the most attractive summer resort between Salem and Gloucester. It boasts every variety of attractions On one side is as good a bathing beach as the coast affords, and a cove for the anchorage of yachts. On the other is "a stern and rock-bound" coast, backed by a dense forest. In front, is Massachusetts bay, with its fishing grounds and islands, and innumerable sail. The woods of which we have spoken are threaded by countless footpaths, which lead to pleasant groves, or to the bluff shore ; while a good carriage road extends through towards Gloucester. Berries and wild flowers greet us on every hand, and back in the neighboring swamp grows the fragrant magnolia, whose perfume permeates the evening air for miles around. "The Flume," about a half mile from the hotels, is a channel in the cliff, 150 feet in length, 50 feet in depth, and 6 feet in width, with perpendicular sides. Rafe's chasm, a little way beyond, is another attractive "natural curiosity." It is a channel cut into the solid rock, nearly 60 feet in depth, 200 feet in length, and 10 feet in width. During a storm the water rushes into this channel with tremendous force, striking against its sides with the sound of thunder, and spouting upwards in torrents. The reef of Norman's woe is an island rock a short distance from the high cliffs of the mainland. It was here, tradition says, that the schooner Hesperus was wrecked in the latter part of the seventeenth century. The probate records of Essex county show that a Richard Norman, about 1680, sailed on a voyage from which he never returned, and if the tradition is founded upon fact, the tragic termination of his voyage was probably on this reef. Longfellow in his "Wreck of the Hesperus," tells how, while

> "The snow fell hissing in the brine,
> And the billows frothed like yeast,"

the skipper, who had "taken his little daughter to bear him company,"

> " Wrapped her warm in his seaman's coat,
>   Against the stinging blast ;
> He cut a rope from a broken spar,
>   And bound her to the mast."

The father froze to death ; then :—

> "And fast through the midnight dark and drear,
>   Through the whistling sleet and snow,
> Like a sheeted ghost the vessel swept
>   Tow'rds the reef of Norman's Woe.
>
> She struck where the white and fleecy waves
>   Looked soft as carded wool,
> But the cruel rocks, they gored her side
>   Like the horns of an angry bull.
>
> At day-break, on the bleak sea-beach,
>   A fisherman stood aghast,
> To see the form of a maiden fair,
>   Lashed close to a drifting mast.
>
> The salt sea was frozen on her breast,
>   The salt tears in her eyes ;
> And he saw her hair, like the brown sea-weed,
>   On the billows fall and rise.
>
> Such was the wreck of the Hesperus,
>   In the midnight and the snow !
> Christ save us all from a death like this,
>   On the reef of Norman's Woe !"

Those who visit this reef, or the shore along here, should not approach too near the water, for it is very deceptive, and often springs up the rocks unexpectedly. People have been washed off and drowned, and the iron cross here marks the spot where the body of Miss Marvin was laid after being taken from the water, in 1879, an unexpectedly high wave having washed her away. Besides the highway and the railway, Magnolia may, at some seasons of the year, be reached by boat. The railroad station is about a mile from the point, but lines of barges connect with all trains. The regular lines of barges at the Magnolia station are run by Gorham Davis and A. J. Rowe. Mr. Davis also keeps a stable at the point. The Glouces-

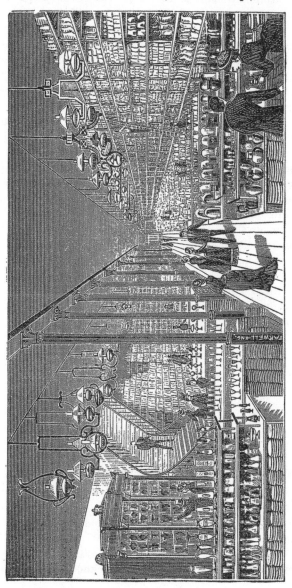

ter boats frequently touch here in summer, and sometimes boats run from Salem. With the growth of the place the frequency and regularity of the boat trips will increase. If now we return to the Gloucester road and drive for about two miles through the woods, we shall emerge at the head of Fresh-water cove, an inlet from Gloucester outer harbor. The English villa on the right, with lawns sloping away to the edge of the cove is "Brook Bank," the residence of Mr. Samuel E. Sawyer who gave a liberal sum to found a public library in Gloucester, and for whom the library is named. The avenue now extends along the side of the hill, the trees and houses far above us on the left, and the ocean sixty or seventy feet below on the right. On one of these cliffs above is the cottage occupied by the family of the late Eben Dale. Between here and the town is some attractive natural scenery, and among the handsome residences is that of John Bray, on the next hill, to the right. Instead of following the avenue the traveler should enter the field on the shore side and drive along the carriage path past old Stage Fort. This is supposed to be the site of the first settlement on Cape Ann. There is little doubt but that Conant's "large frame house" which was moved to Salem, was built near where the old breastwork now is.

GLOUCESTER.

BRIEF HISTORY OF THE CITY—EXTENT OF ITS FISHERIES. BASS ROCKS—EAST GLOUCESTER — ANNISQUAM — BAY VIEW—SOME BUSINESS HOUSES.

Gloucester is 31 miles from Boston, and at the head of Gloucester harbor. Its Indian name was Wingærsheek. The first settlement was effected here by Roger Conant about 1624 for fishing and farming purposes. He and his followers abandoned it in 1626 and part went to Salem; the others returned to England. The historian Babson thinks a permanent settlement was effected about 1633. In 1642, a plantation was incorporated by the name of Gloucester. A church was organized under Rev. Richard Blymman, probably in 1643. John Emerson, the third minister, was paid "60 pounds per annum in Indian corn, peas, barley, fish, mackerel, beef or pork." He served 40 years or more. Rev. John White, who succeeded him, was ordained April 21, 1709. He died at the age of 83, having served as pastor of this church 58 years. In the year 1743, the population having outgrown the agricultural capacity of the place, a number of young men emigrated to a township in Maine about twenty miles from Portland which they named New Gloucester in honor of the parent town. Among the citizens of the new town we may now find the names of some of the earlier settlers at Cape Ann, such as Eveleth, Grover, Haskell, Nevens, (then Evans), Skellin (now Skillings), Fogg, Rowe, Wharff, Witham and others. Our municipal history of Gloucester may be closed with its incorporation as a city on April 28, 1873, and the inauguration of Robert R. Fears as the first mayor in 1874. Its population by the United States census of 1880 was 19,288. The town of Gloucester originally included the entire portion of the headland on the northerly side of Massachusetts bay, known as Cape Ann and also a portion of nearly equal extent running back on the cape to Manchester. The present city is divided into six distinct villages, East Gloucester; Annisquam on the north side of the Cape; Bay View, Lanesville; West Gloucester, and Gloucester village, or city proper, which borders on the harbor. Gloucester is noted especially for two things: For being the largest fishing port in the United States; and as the place where Universalism was really founded as a religious denomination. The doctrine was first preached here in 1774, and the first religious body in America professing the doctrine of universal salvation was organized by John Murray on January 1, 1779. The church was on what is now the corner of Spring and Water streets.

The fishing industry was first actively pursued in the eighteenth century. In 1841 it had so increased that seventy fishing vessels were owned in the town. In 1875 the number had increased to eighty of an aggregate tonnage of 4,000 tons, and an average value of $1,400. Besides these fishermen in distant waters, some seventy vessels were employed in fishing in home waters. The figures of the fishing business in 1873 are as follows: Cod fish, 460,000 quintals, valued at $2,070,000; other fish, 25,000 quintals, valued at $50,000; fresh fish, including halibut, 9,000,000 pounds, valued at $310,000; oil, 275,000 gallons, valued at $165,000; mackerel, 86,544 barrels, valued at $1,125,000; herring, 5,000 barrels, valued at $23,000; shell-fish, 18,000 barrels, valued at $18,000; miscellaneous, $40,000; total value of the fisheries for the year 1873, $3,800,000. There were 375 vessels with 3500 men engaged in the business that year. The figures for 1876 were: Cod, $2,020,297; halibut, $679,954; mackerel, $710,201.* These figures are ample to indicate the enormous extent of the fishing business of this port. This work, as all know, is attended with very great danger, nearly as great as that of active service in the army in the time of war. Since 1830, 250 or more vessels and more than 1800 lives have been lost in the fisheries. During the year 1873, alone, 31 vessels and 174 lives were lost.

The tower of the City hall, St. Anne's (catholic) church and the wharves should be visited, if nothing else is. From the tower of the city hall a grand view is obtained of the city, the surrounding country and the harbor and ocean. St. Anne's church was begun in 1876 and completed, save the tower, in 1880. It is a pure gothic edifice. It is rectangular in form, 78 by 142 feet, with a spire (when completed) 180 feet in height. The windows are of beautiful, stained glass, while the ceiling and walls are artistically frescoed, the various niches bearing some sterling figures emblematic of the faith. The altar is of the richest marble of different colors, from Italy, Spain, France and other countries—and of pure Gothic. Behind and above it the four great windows contain figures of Our Blessed Lord, the Virgin Mary, St. Joseph and St Anne. Two smaller altars stand on either side. The painting on the left of the main altar is one of the finest works of art in this country. It represents the mother of John the Baptist taking him to see the young Christ. On the opposite wall is a fine painting representing the " Adoration of the Magi." Both were done at the Pitti palace in Florence under direction of Father Healey. The wharves and fish-packing houses will be found interesting and instructive. The station of the Eastern railway is on the northerly side of the city. It was built in 1878. Cars leave here for Rockport and for Salem, Boston and other points seven times each day. Coaches depart for East Gloucester, Bay View and Lanesville on arrival of the trains.

Among the business houses to which we desire to call attention are Alex. Pattilio's dry goods establishment; A. J. Rowe's livery stables and the copper paint manufacturies of Tarr and Wonson and James H. Tarr, the two latter mentioned below. Mr. Pattilio's house was burnt out in the great fire in 1864, again in 1870, and yet again in 1872, but has risen each time only to improve wherever improvement is possible. Mr. Rowe keeps a fine large stable well supplied with every description of vehicles and a plenty of good horses. He also has a stable at Magnolia.

THE EAST GLOUCESTER section of the town is sub-divided into East Gloucester village, Bass Rocks and Eastern Point. The first named is composed of the modest cottages occupied by the families of fishermen. There are also a few shops for the manufacture, of various articles used in the fisheries. There are two extensive manufactories of copper paint here: those of Tarr & Wonson and James H. Tarr. This is a paint composed mainly of ground copper and tar mixed, and is used to paint the bottoms of vessels. At the manufactory of Tarr & Wonson an immense business is done. The copper is ground, dried, and mixed by machinery. From the time it disappears in the mill until it goes in the tin cans, ready for use, it is not handled at all. During this time it has passed from the second floor to the first; then back to the second, then to the first again, next to the basement where it is mixed, and lastly is pumped to the second floor, where it is canned.

On the ocean side of East Gloucester is the delightful summer resort known as BASS ROCKS AND GOOD HARBOR BEACH. We may go by stage or by private carriage, leaving

the city by way of East Main street. From the elevation
between East Gloucester village and Bass Rocks we obtain a
fine view of the surroundings. Below us lie the city and the
harbor with its shipping, and the fishing vessels going and
coming. Back of this picture, across the harbor and town, is
nature's setting of granite hills and dense woods, broken here
and there by a green field. If the day be clear, we see the
Cape Ann shore toward Salem, then Salem harbor, the bay,
Half-way rock, Marblehead with the tall tower of Abbot Hall,
old Boston light, and the South Shore with its burning sands,
in striking contrast with the cool green hills of the North
Shore. Away to the right, towards Essex, is Beacon Pole hill.
On the ocean side is the broad Atlantic, unbroken save by the
numerous white sail. A little to the left lie Salt island, Milk
island and Thatchers island. Turning into Beach avenue, we
pass the Bass Rock House and proceed to Little Good Harbor
beach. The land hereabouts was formerly the property of the
late George H. Rogers. Mr. Rogers expended about a hundred
thousand dollars in improving the land and bringing it into the
market because he knew that in time it would become a popular sea-shore resort. His prediction has been fulfilled, but he
did not live to realize his hopes. When he died the Gloucester
Land company bought the property and sold some twenty or
more lots on which residences were built. The Bass Rocks
House was also one of the improvements of this company.
Subsequently Mr. Henry Souther, of South Boston, bought
the entire estate including the hotel and unsold building lots,
and set about improving the place and peopling it. The location is peculiarly adapted to the intended use. The land slopes
away to the ocean and the high elevation renders it free from
all impurities such as poor drainage and marshes.

The Bass Rock House, the only hotel hereabouts, was opened
by Mrs. E. G. Brown in 1879, and has been a success from the
start. It enjoys one of the coolest locations on the cape and
as a health resort is unsurpassed. From its piazzas a magnificent view is obtained of Massachusetts bay and the surrounding country. The cut represents the buildings as they appeared
in 1879. Two stories and a broad piazza have since been added,
and the dining room enlarged and reconstructed, giving it a

capacity for seating 140 guests. The beach is crescent shaped, about three-quarters of a mile in length, and the finest on the cape for surf and still water bathing. It is free from under-tow, and perfectly safe at any time of tide. The Bass Rock House is noted for the excellence of its cuisine, and has a select class of patronage. Those wishing a quiet home-like

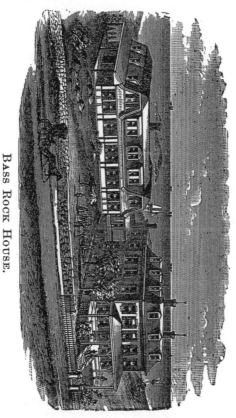

BASS ROCK HOUSE.

lace by the sea, will find here all that can be desired, away from the annoyance of a crowd of transient people and excursionists. A book, entitled "A summer Resort on Cape Ann," can be obtained on application to Mrs. Brown.

Some excellent drives radiate from Gloucester. We may drive to Magnolia and Salem, or in the opposite direction to

Eastern point, over roads already described; or we may drive
to Rockport village and Pigeon Cove on the one side, or Annisquam, Bay View and Lanesville on the other; or we may
drive entirely around the cape, a distance of about eighteen
miles. If the visitor drives in either of the two last named
directions he should not confine himself to the highway but
enter some of the better conditioned quarry roads and drives
around them. Many of these roads are in good condition and
lead through striking scenery. Care should be taken when
visiting quarries not to get too near the blasts, as there is great
danger. If we are going to Bay View and vicinity we leave
Gloucester by Washington street, passing the cemetery on the
right. The first place of interest is the little settlement of
Riverdale with its old mill, pretty stream and thrifty looking
farms. A mile beyond we turn to the left and cross Annisquam river to the village of the same name, but commonly
called Squam. Time was when more vessels fitted from here
than from Gloucester. On the hill back of the village is the
Cambridge settlement, so-called because most of the summer
residents are Cambridge people. The view from the top of this
hill is one of the best on the Cape. The residences are mainly
pretty cottages, although Isaac Adams, the patentee of the
nickel-plating process, has a costly mansion at the summit
of the hill, and Curtis Davis and W. B. Hastings on Cambridge
avenue. The only hotel is the small Highland House.
From Annisquam to Bay View is some two miles.

Bay View is among the most widely known sections
of the Cape, because of General Butler's connection with
it. He has a summer residence and used to pass much of
his time here. His house stands on the left as we enter the
village, Col. Jonas H. French's being the first. Both are of
granite. Gen. Butler's has not received much care of late,
but Col. French's is a most charming retreat. The prospect
from the piazza of his house is unusually good, commanding
as it does Ipswich bay and all that line of coast to New
Hampshire. The Cape Ann granite company's works here
should be visited. Col. French is president of the company.
H. H. Bennett, treasurer, and Scott Webber, superintendent.
There are two distinct quarries worked by this company; one

a half mile from the street, and the other about a mile. The present proprietors purchased this land in 1869, and began work in April of the same year. The company employs from 300 to 600 men, according to the business on hand.

The process of quarrying stone is something like this: The soil being cleared from a ledge and an examination having been made to see how the seams run, a steam drill is set to work boring two holes from 10 to 18 feet in depth and three inches in width, and two inches apart. A half keg of powder is put in these holes, and ignited with electrictity. The explosion lifts the ledge from seam to seam, usually in a straight line. Sometimes these lifts are of 20,000 tons weight. The blasts do not smash the rocks at all; a person is perfectly safe standing a few feet away. The section of the ledge thus broken off is split into smaller sections, to suit various purposes, with small hand drills and wedges. These pieces are taken to the yard by a train of cars, there to be worked into whatever shape desired, with hammer and chisel. The work is mainly done from drawings, though sometimes from patterns. The pieces of stone for the various purposes are entirely prepared at the company's yard, so that there is no cutting or trimming when they arrive at their destination; nothing to do but put them in place. The largest block ever taken out was that for the platform of the Scott monument at Washington, which in its rough state weighed 150¾ tons. When finished and ready for shipment it weighed 119 tons. Among the more prominent structures composed wholly or in part of Bay View granite are the U. S. post office and sub-treasury, Boston; the approaches to the patent office and post office in Washington; the military academy at West Point; monument and tower to Miles Standish at Duxbury; the new public library at Philadelphia; the spandrels of the New York and Brooklyn bridge.

Salem Music Store.

WALLIS & YOUNG,

201 ESSEX STREET.

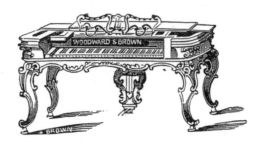

FIRST CLASS

Pianos & Organs

Rented and Sold at Prices as Low as the Lowest.

And Perfect Satisfaction Guaranteed.

☞ We are agents for the celebrated **Estey Organs**, noted for their pure silver-like tone and durability. Also everything found in a First Class Music Store.

Strings of the Best Quality, for all Instruments.
Violins, Guitars, Banjos, Flutes, &c.

Stationery and Fancy Goods.

Trimmings for all kinds of Instruments.

PIANOS and ORGANS Tuned and Repaired.

At the Salem Music Store,

WALLIS & YOUNG, 201 Essex Street,

SALEM, MASS.

Croquet, and Games of the Season.

ROCKPORT.

ITS HISTORY — THATCHER'S ISLAND — PIGEON COVE — OCEAN VIEW POINT—DESCRIPTION OF A STORM.

Rockport is the last town on Cape Ann. It is most appropriately named, for it is a port and a rocky one in the fullest sense. The depot, the terminus of the Cape Ann branch of the Eastern, is four miles from Gloucester and 35.4 miles from Boston. The railway and highway pass through a largely uninhabited section, the old Beaver dam farm being the only interruption of the wilderness. "Great" hill, just beyond the farm is a sightly place. The bay and village and Pigeon Cove and village lie before us in the distance; to the left are hills of rock and forest,— Pool's hill, Thompson's mountain and Pigeon hill. Amid these rise the tall derricks of the great granite quarries. To the right lies the open sea with its islands, rocks and white sails.

A drive through the village and out Mt. Pleasant street brings us very near to Straitsmouth island and light at the entrance to Rockport harbor, and to the famous lighthouses on Thatcher's island, those familiar beacons, like sturdy sentinels, standing guard for Cape Ann. Babson says this island was purchased by Rev. John White for 100 pounds. He sold it to Joseph Allen in 1727 for 175 pounds. In 1771 the colonial government became its owner at a cost of 500 pounds, and proceeded in the same year to erect two lighthouses and a dwelling house on it. The lamps were lighted for the first time on Dec. 21, 1771. The old lighthouses were supplanted by the present noble structures a few years ago. Henry C. Leonard, in his little work on Pigeon Cove, says, "the sea-birds, attracted by the splendor of these quenchless flames, fly with such force against the plates of glass which protect the

flames from wind and storm, that they fall dead upon the
rocks around the towers.''

> "The rocky ledge runs far out into the sea,
>   And on its outer point some miles away,
> The lighthouse lifts its massive masonry,
>   A pillar of fire by night, a cloud by day.
>
> Like the great Christopher it stands,
>   Upon the brink of the tempestuous wave,
> Wading far out among the rocks and sands,
>   The night o'ertaken mariner to save.
>
> Steadfast, serene, immovable, the same
>   Year after year, through all the silent night,
> Burns on forevermore that quenchless flame,
>   Shines on that inextinguishable light.
>
> The sea-bird wheeling round it, with the din
>   Of wings, and winds, and solitary cries,
> Blinded and maddened with the light within,
>   Dashes himself against the glass and dies.''

The town was settled by John Babson, (1695,) and Richard
Tarr, (1697,) the former at Straitsmouth and the latter
where the village now stands. At the breaking out of the
Revolutionary war, seventy Rockport boats were engaged in the
fisheries, about as large a number as there has ever been since.
The government began to build a breakwater at Long cove in
1836, but abandoned the work for the want of money in 1840.
The population increased from about 400 in 1775 to 704 in 1792
and 2,650 in 1840. In the last named year the inhabitants,
after much opposition from the parent town of Gloucester,
were set off as an independent municipality under the name
of Rockport. The first town meeting was held on March 9 of
that year. Col. Pool held the office of clerk continuously until
1868, when he resigned and was succeeded by his son, Calvin
W. Pool, the present incumbent. The most remunerative
interest at the present time is granite cutting. Nature be-
stowed upon Rockport a rich mine in the great granite ledges,
an apparently inexhaustible quarry from which generation
after generation will draw wealth. Granite was first cut from
these hills in 1710, to construct mooring stones for fishermen;
not, however, until the beginning of the nineteenth century
were stones cut and used for building purposes. The value o

the granite quarried in Rockport and the section of Gloucester adjoining must be several hundred thousand dollars.

Our interest, however, centres in Pigeon Cove and vicinity, the far-famed summer resort. The journey can be made by coach, the distance being two miles. These coaches connect with every train. The fares are 25 cents each way. A railroad is needed to the Cove and will be built sometime, no doubt. The principal hotel is the *Pigeon Cove House*, kept by Mrs. Ellen S. Robinson since 1866. The praises of this house and its location have been sung from New England to the Pacific, and from Canada to Texas. The present building was erected in 1871 by Mrs. Robinson. She also owns the Sea View House near by, but does not manage it. Mrs. Robinson has devoted the best years of her life to the management of summer hotels at the North and winter hotels at the South. How faithfully she has served her patrons thousands can testify. The house has seventy-five sleeping rooms besides offices, dining rooms and elegant parlors. There are also several private boarding and lodging houses in the immediate vicinity.

Just beyond the cove is Ocean View point, the extreme end of Cape Ann. There are three principal avenues leading thither—Phillips, northern and southern sections, and Babson avenue between the two. The property here comprises the entire projection of land constituting the northeasterly section of Rockport, a territory of some fifty acres, formerly known as "the Allen pasture." Byrant once wrote:—"No place of resort by the sea-side in New England has such forest attractions as Pigeon Cove. The woods look like a beautiful temple." The late Dr. Chapin said, "The ocean view is one of the grandest I have ever seen." It is certainly an interesting spectacle to witness the ocean from this point, during a storm. The scene is marvelously grand; it is awe-inspiring; it is sublime. Though the writer has witnessed it often, it is impossible to portray the picture more faithfully than does the following article written by a lady correspondent of the New Orleans Times, in 1877:

For three days they have had such tides as have not beaten on these rocks for seven years! A—— and I have lived out of doors. Our hats have been on our heads from morning till

night, and the rocks have known us "from early morn till
dewy eve." There has been a sort of fascination in the sight
for us, and while we gazed and never tired of gazing, we were
all the while conscious how utterly inadequate all language
was to convey any idea of the awful sublimity of the scene.
It has not rained; and although a northeast wind was blowing
most of the time, if properly wrapped it was not at all uncom-
fortable for those on the shore. In fact, Saturday was the only
day really worthy of being called chilly. Yesterday the sun
shone, the temperature was delightful, with the noblest seas
running that we have yet had. The scene along the whole
coast as far as the eye could reach was sublime Every projecting rock was a point at which a fountain of milk-white
spray leaped forty or fifty feet in the air, and every billow
sweeping up the shore left the rock foaming with waterfalls and
cascades, which went frothing and swirling back toward the
deep, never reaching it before another wave broke and replaced
the fugitive torrent. In the chasms and rifts and gullies all
was boiling, seething foam, and here and there in some broad
ravine's mouth, where the wind and tide met and battled, all
was "confusion worse confounded" and seemed as if hell-broth
were brewing in a cauldrons tirred by mad witches Upon the
stones facing the sea, the terrible magnificence of the scene
struck one dumb. Far out from the shore the waves could be
seen to rise, and growing as they rose, take up their awful
march toward the land. As they drew near, they seemed like
gigantic sea monsters which reared and pawed the air in sav-
age wrath, then with a fearful noise flung themselves upon
the solid stones, which with calm defiance met the shock.
From point to point one wandered along the rocks, each new
view seeming grander than the last, everywhere groups of persons could be seen gazing upon the riotous waters. There
was a general seeking for companionship; no one seemed to
wish to be alone, for a certain degree of terror was mingled
with the awe and admiration the scene excited. Seated upon
the rocks, thirty feet above the water level, we watch the
gathering billows. They sweep toward us—swell, roar—then
dash upon the shore, breaking into countless cataracts, and
filling the air with spray; as we see them come, the bravest

holds his breath. Involuntarily one grasps his neighbor and
shrinks back; then with a gasp and a shudder, he sees the
volume of water disperse, and spell-bound fixes his gaze upon
the next wave. The noise and tumult meanwhile are that of
two or three Niagaras, and where the water is driven against
certain forms of rock loud reports are heard like the regular
shock of artillery. Hissing as if the rocks were red hot,
the white lips of the waves kiss the stones, while the
splash and splatter of the uptossed water is dropping
everywhere. Above all the ceaseless swish and swirm
and rush and riot of the maddened seas one hears
another and almost appalling sound. It is like the distant
roll of underground thunder. It seems to come from the
very throat of the hoarse deep, and the earth feels its vibra-
tions. It is a sound of the sea which yet seems distinct from
the sea, and falls upon the ear like a threat, ominous of some
dire thing to come, yet more terrible than any. Passing up to
the extreme point of the cape, entirely a new scene presents
itself. Here instead of rushing at the shore like rearing uni-
corns, the rollers stretch themselves out from north to south,
and roll westward. We see them built, as by magic, far out;
they rise, great walls of green water; borne forward by invisi-
ble hands, they resolve themselves into mighty cylinders of
malachite, millions upon millions of pale demons, robed in foam
and spray, dance and revel, and hold mad orgies, until, suddenly
losing hold, they slip from the green summit and go headlong
down the grassy surge, which, suddenly shattered, sweeps past
in its shivered splendor, and is hurled against the shore a chaos
of froth and fury—of amber, emerald and pearl. As the eye
goes back toward the sea, it beholds a strange army advancing.

They are old men of the sea—Druids of the deep—their robes
are woven of emerald water, their long beards are like snow,
and their hair, whiter than the thrice-washed fleece, floats out
upon the wind. From their shoulders hang feathery mantles
of spotless white, and they march forward with the calm
courage born of a belief in their own invincibility, till, suddenly catching sight of the stern foe in rocky silence waiting
them on shore, they fall prostrate on their faces—their white
mantles cover them—their white hair tosses and tangles in the

gale—the great deep swallows them up—and the eye seeks them
in vain in the tumultuous meadows of the sea. Amid countless
interruptions, I have feebly given you some idea of the scene
with only one regret, viz: that more of my New Orleans
friends were not here to share the picture. In it I found am-
ple reward for my long journey by land and water, and my
determined purpose to reach "Pigeon Cove." This "stern and
rock-bound coast" is to me a source of endless interest. I
drink in draughts of briny air; I watch the changes of light
upon the water, the colors of the rocks on shore, and search
eagerly among the weeds and mosses brought up from the mys-
terious gardens of the deep for some sea flower which I may
keep as a memento of this time.

The only hotel at the point is the *Linwood*. Its location is

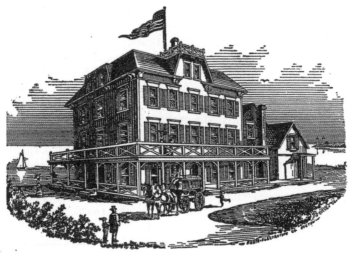

LINWOOD HOUSE.

one of the most romantic and picturesque on the coast. It
stands within two hundred feet of the water, on a high cliff
overlooking the ocean, with Massachusetts bay on one side and
Ipswich bay on the other. From the top of the house the
panorama is grand beyond description. The whole shore
to Rockport village, and, beyond it, Straitsmouth and Thatch-

er's on one side, the Salvages, and the open sea in front, and the white sands of Ipswich bay, Mt. Agamenticus and the Isles of Shoals, on the other, are plainly visible. The house is of recent and modern construction, and is heated by furnace. Mr. James Hurd is proprietor.

The distinctive feature of Rockport as a Summer resort, is its picturesqueness. Some striking scene greets one on every hand. If it is not the wild war of the waves on a stormy day, it is the charm of the walks in the woods and among the old granite quarries on a summer morning. America affords few places where such charming wood-walks exist. Col. Higginson says:—" The whole interior of Cape Ann, beyond Gloucester, is a continuous woodland, with granite ledges everywhere cropping out, around which the high-road winds, following the curving and indented line of the sea, and dotted here and there with fishing hamlets. This whole interior is traversed by a network of foot paths, rarely passable for a wagon, and not always for a horse, but enabling the pedestrian to go from any one of these villages to any other, in a line almost direct, and always under an agreeable shade."* If one is driving through this section, he will, after leaving Pigeon Cove, proceed around the shore by Folly point and Halibut point, and, passing through a lovely arch of willows enter the little village of Lanesville in Gloucester. The road to this point is usually in good condition, although, as may be supposed, it is winding and uneven. Here we take leave of that wonderful and charming section of New England known as Cape Ann.

---

* Oldport Days, p. 251.

4

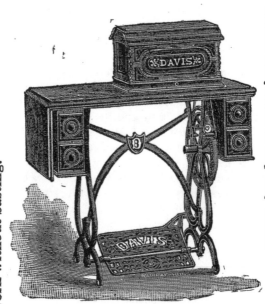

IPSWICH.

A Charming Country Town—Its Interesting History — Hills and Valleys — Heartbreak Hill — Town Hill—Business Directory.

The beautiful town of Ipswich is 28 miles from Boston and 12 from Salem, on the line of the Eastern railway. It is here that the double track ends; beyond, there is only a single track. In all New England it would be difficult to find a settlement which more forcibly reminds one of the typical modern English country town. The houses are large and many of them somewhat old-fashioned—sort of grand and imposing like. The elms, however, are what give the place that English look. They are the growth of many generations and their wide spreading branches span the exceptionally broad streets. Some of these trees are six feet in diameter. Ipswich roads are broad, winding, undulating and as smooth as a house floor. The whole air of the town bespeaks dignity and solidity, as if it had come down from many a distant generation wearing all its honors. And, yet, unlike Marblehead it has none of that weather-beaten, antique appearance. Everything is moderately bright and fresh. Few people, doubtless, are aware that the Mayflower came near landing her now historic freight of humanity at Ipswich. The vessel was anchored off the bar and a boat sent out to prospect, but the sea was rough and it returned without effecting a landing. Had the Pilgrims landed here we should never have had Mrs. Heman's "A stern and rockbound coast," because there are no rocks on this coast. Ipswich was settled in 1633. Its Indian name was Agawam. John Winthrop, jr., bought the plantation of the Indian chief Masconomo, in 1638, for £20. The first meeting house was built in 1634. Rev. Nathaniel Ward, author of the tract, "The Simple Cobbler of Aggawam," was the pastor. The town was incorporated in the same year. In 1793, Ipswich hamlet was detached and incorporated as the town of Hamilton. In 1819, the second parish of Ipswich was incorporated as the town of Essex. In 1846, a section of the town was added to Boxford. The population in 1870 was 3,720; in 1875, 3,674; in 1880, 3,702; it has increased during the past year. The industries are farming, shoe making and the manufacture of hosiery and woolen goods. The hosiery mill gives employment to above 400 people and the monthly pay roll averages $12,000. Ipswich is noted for its orchards and hay farms. It is one of the most extensive hay growing towns in the commonwealth. Its agricultural productions in 1875 exceeded those of any other town in Essex county. There are five churches in the village: The North Congregational, on the "Green;" the South Congregational, on the South side; the Methodist, on Common street; the Catholic, towards Prospect hill and the Episcopal, on County street. The village has schools, halls, offices and stores to an unusual degree for a country town. There are two common schools and the Manning high school. The latter was built in 1873-4, with a fund of $35,-000 left by the late Dr. Thomas Manning. His nephew, Richard H. Manning, of Brooklyn, gave $15,000 and Hon. J. G. Cogswell, of New York, $4,000 additional. The cabinet of natural curiosities, mineral and botanical specimens is probably the best in the county after that at Salem. The town has a splendid free public library,—the Heard library,—of about 8,000 volumes. It is on Common street and was established on a fund of $18,000 left by Augustine Heard. He also left books and other property, making his whole donation $50,000. Daniel Treadwell of Cambridge, a native of Ipswich, gave his library and other property, amounting in all to $20,000, to the same institution. The first newspaper in town was the Ipswich Journal, started in 1827. It was short-lived. The Chronicle was started in 1872, by E. L. Davenport, and is now owned by Daniels & Potter. It is a newsy sheet. There are lodges of Odd Fellows, Masons and Good Templars in the town. One of the county houses of correction and an insane asylum are located back of the village. Two stone bridges span Ipswich river. Choate bridge on Main street was built in 1764, at a cost of £1,000 and the other, on County street in 1861.

Ipswich has furnished some really "great men" in the field of letters and jurisprudence. Nathan Dane, member of Congress, author of Dane's Abridgement of American law and founder of the Dane professorship at Harvard, was born here. Also, J. C. Perkins, who died in Salem, served on the court of common pleas, and wrote many works on law; Hon. Otis P. Lord, of Salem, now a justice of the supreme judicial court; Nathaniel Appleton, minister and lawyer, and judge of the probate court for 20 years; John G. Cogswell, for many years librarian of the Astor library and an intimate friend of George Bancroft; Gen. Wm. Sutton, now of Peabody, well known throughout the state.

So much for the history of the town. Now a word descriptive. Ipswich has some features peculiar to itself. Nowhere else do we find such noble, round, smooth hills. They rise in every direction, like ant-hills on a sandy lawn. Between them are beautiful green valleys, while on the ocean side are vast meadows and marshes. The hills are free from rocks, and the soil is remarkably fertile and productive. It is a combination of fine gravel and loam which works well in the field and treads in the road like so much adamant. Ipswich river, the prettiest stream of water in the county, drains the town and the section to the north. The water is very dark, almost black from the rich soil, yet pure and clear as crystal. This stream terminates in Ipswich bay. At the village it falls several feet, and just beyond the county houses it meets tide water, the head of navigation. From the village to the bay is some two miles, and the river pursues a winding course through the meadows. A trip "down river" is considered the finest treat which Ipswich people can offer to their visitors, and certainly it would not be an easy matter to find a pleasanter. The pretty steamer Carlotta, Capt. Burnham, plys back and forth during the summer. Inquire for his boat. Beyond this is a vast sandbar over which the water breaks into milk-white spray.

There is a legend that one Harry Main, an early settler, was, because of a blasphemous act, chained to this bar with an iron shovel and sentenced to shovel back the sand for a thousand years. So when the sea roars the people say:

"Harry Main has had hard work to-day." Such is the legend, but probably no one believes it, any more than they do that the town voted at one and the same time to tear down the stone bridge and build a new one of the same stone, and "to use the old bridge while the new one was being built." The shore at the mouth of the river trends away on either hand, the same low white line of fine sand. The facilities for salt-water bathing could not well be better. This beach terminates at Annisquam river after being cut across by Essex and Chebacco rivers. North of here Plum island stretches away for nine miles, another unbroken line of sand, to the very entrance of Newburyport harbor. But of all the features of the town none are so striking as the great round-topped hills. The most popular one in many respects is Town hill which lies just back of the village. It rises abruptly from High street to a height of some two hundred feet above the level of the sea. The view from its summit is unsurpassed in all this section. Beginning with the Danvers Insane Asylum to the South-west we find next in line toward the ocean, the village of Hamilton and in the foreground, the winding Ipswich river. A mile further to the east is the Candlewood district in Ipswich. Far away in the distance is the Manchester and Essex woods and a range of hills in Essex which hides the town from us. Nearer, and to the left, is Heartbreak hill. There is a legend connected with this hill. Celia Thaxter tells it in her beautiful poem:

"In Ipswich town, not far from the sea,
    Rises a hill which the people call
Heartbreak hill, and its history
    Is an old, old legend known to all."

The legend is told in the third and last verses of a poem of sixteen stanzas.

"It was a sailor who won the heart
    Of an Indian maiden, lithe and strong,
And she saw him over the sea depart,
    While sweet in her ear his promise rang.
        *   *   *   *   *   *   *
He never came back! Yet faithful still
    She watched from the hilltop her life away;
And the towns people christened it Heartbreak hill,
    And it bears the name to this very day."

Still another range of hills stretches away from here to the very water's edge. This is the Castle hill range. What a magnificent location for a summer hotel! Behind Castle hill is Hog island, the birth-place of Rufus Choate. This island is situated in the middle of Essex river. In the distance we see the Cape Ann shore, Annisquam and Bay View. The water at the base of Castle hill is of sufficient depth to float large vessels. Crossing the mouth of the river we have Little neck and Great neck, both parts of a bold headland which from the water seems to rise perpendicularly out of the ocean. Beyond all these objects we behold the broad ocean for 75 miles with its numerous sails, from Cape Ann to the distant coast of Maine. The Isles of Shoals and Mt. Agamenticus are distinctly visible from this hill. Another turn to the left and we see the spires of Newburyport, Amesbury and Rowley. Ipswich village is three miles to the northwest, between two of those great hills. In the same direction are Turkey hill, and Bartholomew hill; and directly west, Turner hill, noticeable for a line of trees on one side, like so many silent sentinels. This completes the circle around our location on Town hill. A more sightly place or grander views are rarely found. The wonder is that this hill has not all been built upon years ago. There is not a better location for summer residences in all Essex county. The health of the place is undisputed, because the opportunities for drainage are perfect. In the very centre of this hill, on the land owned by J. B. Wells, is a beautiful tiny pond of pure water. At very small cost a good reservoir might be constructed here and the whole town supplied with water. A street has been begun, to extend between Spring and High streets, directly over the summit of Town hill. It will be 60 feet in width and lined with shade trees. There can be no question as to the future of this place. It cannot possibly remain unoccupied much longer. The immediate sea-shore along our coast is practically all occupied, and the nex step must be in the direction of the elevated land back from the shore. Considering that suburban residences are now occupied from early spring to late fall, it is a question whether a few miles removed from the water is not desirable. In fact, this change is already taking place along the Cape Ann shore, and the eligible locations are fast being brought into market. Those who are seeking for a building spot will be wise if they include this hill and the town of Ipswich in their tour of inspection.

The *Eastern International House*, kept by Mrs. Mary Smith, is on Central street, just beyond the Manning school building. This is the principal hotel of the town. Mrs. Smith kept the dining rooms at the depot for many years, and it would be difcult to tell how many thousands of hungry travellers have received comfort to the inner man at the old International. Who, that on a cold winter day has been warmed by that familiar notice, "hot muffins," as he entered the room, will ever forget that happy moment ! The house was moved to Central street in 1880, and entirely remodelled and refitted. It has been again repaired and otherwise improved during the spring of 1881. A piazza runs entirely around the house, while the surrounding grounds are prettily laid out. The location is one of the best in town. In fact, few country villages are as fortunate as Ipswich in the matter of hotel accommodations. The International is not alone for transient guests, but for those desirous of passing a week or two of the hot weather in the country.

A list of the principal business houses of the town follows:—on the first floor of Caldwell block, corner of Market and Central streets, we have the spacious pharmacy rooms of Edward F. Brown, formerly for many years occupied by Andrew Geyer. The telegraph office is in his store. On the same floor are David M. Tyler's fine jewelry store and Joseph Johnson's boot and shoe store, both numbered among the town's best business places. Thomas Condon grocer, and George Ellis, shoe dealer, are also located here. In the second story are the offices of the Ipswich Chronicle and Wesley K. Bell, trial justice, and the elegant dental rooms of Dr. J. B. Wells. Dr. Wells has been located in these rooms a long time, which speaks volumes for his popularity and efficiency as a dentist. On Main street, in the vicinity of the First church, we find the Agawam House, an excellent little suburban hotel. Also the well filled dry goods store of Walter Lord, and William Willcomb's confectionery and ice cream store. Opposite, on the other side of the "green", is Odd Fellows block, occupied by Agawam lodge in the upper part, and by the post office and the drug store of John Blake in the lower part. Mr. Blake has the usual assortment of toilet goods. The telephone office is in his store. Maynard Whittier's store is also on Main street. On High street is Asa Lord's grocery store, one of the best in town. On the "south side" of the river, E. Cogswell and son keep a very large variety store, and Stackpole and Son have a large soap manufactory. In Wildes block, near the junction of Market and Main streets, Mr. Higgins has a large and well stocked furniture store, and John A. Newman and E. Plcuff and Son, spacious hardware stores. In the second story we find Dr. A. S. Dudley, the dentist so well known in Salem. In a building adjoining is the periodical store of Mr. Hale, where he keeps all the articles usually found in such an establishment. On Market street we have the spacious dry goods store, of W. S. Russell, one of the best in town. Mr· Russell has kept this store since 1865. Just beyond him, on the same side, is Robert Jordan's tailoring and furnishing goods establishment, the most extensive in the place. Near by is the law office of Charles A. Sayward, Esq., and nearly opposite is John A. Johnson's shoe manufactory. Close by the depot is the immense crockery store of Curtis Damon. It is the largest outside of Salem, if not in Essex county.

A NEW EXCURSION ROUTE.

The authors desire to call attention to one excursion from this section, which may be made cheaply, quickly, and comfortably, and which, although almost unknown among the excursion routes of the day, has some features peculiar to the section alone. We refer to the Aroostook and New Brunswick, along the valley of the St. John. The trip may be made as follows: Leave Boston in the morning over the Eastern, or Boston & Maine; arrive in Bangor at night on the Maine Central; pass the night in Bangor (Bangor House); leave the next morning via the European and North American; dine at Vanceboro; take the New Brunswick and Canada for Woodstock, thence by the New Brunswick & Canada to Fort Fairfield or Caribou; pass the second night here. If desired, the Swedish colony known as New Sweden, nine miles distant, may be visited by carriage. On leaving Caribou return to Fort Fairfield and continue on the main line to Edmandston, and pass the third night; return the next day to Grand Falls, where two days or even a week may well be passed. The return can be made over the same route, or take the New Brunswick and Canada to Fredericton, and thence to St. Andrews, a beautiful seaport town which is destined to become the leading summer resort in the maritime provinces, because of its magnificent and wierd scenery, and remarkably pure and cool atmosphere. It has splendid hotel accommodations, especially at the Argyll, recently built. From St. Andrews return by rail to Bangor. It would be impossible to detail the points of interest on this route. The writers can only say from personal experience that if this excursion is made during the months of July and August, it will be found one of the most interesting in New England and the Canadas. The route takes one through the valleys of the Kennebec, the Penobscot and the St. John rivers, than which nothing finer can be imagined. Grand Falls is one of the most delightful spots in America for a quiet sojourn of a few days or a few weeks. The scenery is superb, and the river below the falls reminds one forcibly of the Canons of Colorado. Board costs from $5 to $10 per week at good hotels. We have deviated thus much from the usual course of this book because this section of the country is almost unknown and because we know every one who visits it will feel grateful for the suggestion.

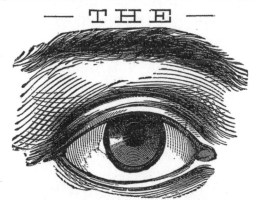

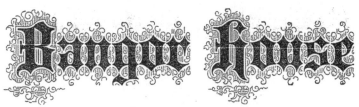

Bangor, Me.

$2.00 PER DAY

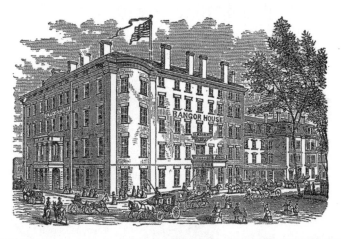

THIS IS one of the BEST HOUSES IN NEW ENGLAND.

It sits in a square by itself, thus avoiding the danger by fire from other buildings, and making every room a front one. It has a brick partition between nearly every room, making it fire-proof.

The Bangor and Mount Desert Stage line leaves the Bangor House every morning (Sundays excepted), at 8 o'clock, arriving at Bar Harbor, Mt. Desert, at 5 P. M., commencing July 5.

F. O. BEAL, Proprietor Bangor House.

FRANK A. BRAGDON,

50 Lowell Street, Peabody,

Manufacturer of Plain and Fancy

CRACKERS,

Biscuits, Wafers, Fancy Cakes, Pilot-Bread, Ship Bread, &c.

Also Manufacturer of the Celebrated

NONPAREIL PILOT BREAD,

— AND —

'SEA FOAM BISCUIT

These two last-named articles will be found to be the *best* that are made, and are indispensable for table use, picnic and excursion parties.

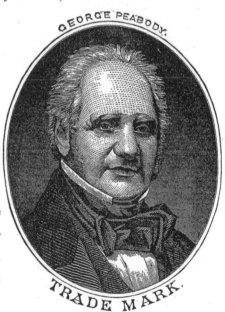

GEORGE PEABODY.

TRADE MARK.

Also Manufacturer of all kinds of

White Bread, Cake and Pastry.

WEDDING and other FANCY CAKE made to order.

All orders by letter or telephone promptly filled.

Sea View House,

MAGNOLIA, MASS.

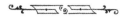

This fine new house offers superior accommodations for twenty-five guests. The location is unsurpassed for healthiness and pleasure. The table is kept up to a high standard throughout the season.

CONNECTED WITH THE HOUSE ARE

Orchard and Croquet Grounds.

Three minutes from the Beach and Bathing Houses.

Terms and other particulars furnished on application to

Mrs. M. C. Honners,

MAGNOLIA, MASS.

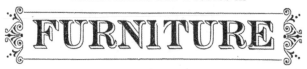
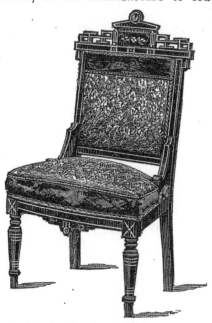

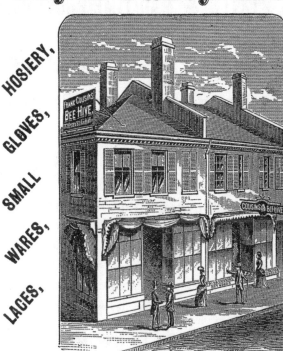

DUDLEY & EWELL,

DENTISTS,

NO. 224 ESSEX STREET, SALEM

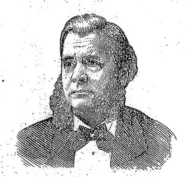

DR. A. S. DUDLEY.

Dr. A. S. Dudley,
16 years in Salem.

Dr. Geo. A. Ewell,
Late of Chicago.

First Class Work.
All Operations Warranted.

TEETH EXTRACTED WITHOUT PAIN.

OUR REFORMED PRICES.

Extracting Teeth, for each Tooth, - - - 25 cts.
" with use of freezing process, - - 50 cts.
" with use of Ether or Gas, - - $1.00

Artificial Teeth of all Styles and Qualities, at moderate prices, and warranted. Prices, from $10 to $35.

Gold Fillings, from $1.00 to $20, according to circumstances.

Platina Fillings, from $1 to $3. Silver and Amalgam, 50 cts. to $1.50. Other fillings from 50 cts. to $1.00.

Terms Cash and No Trust.